OAT
Practice Questions

OAT Practice Tests & Exam Review for the
Optometry Admission Test

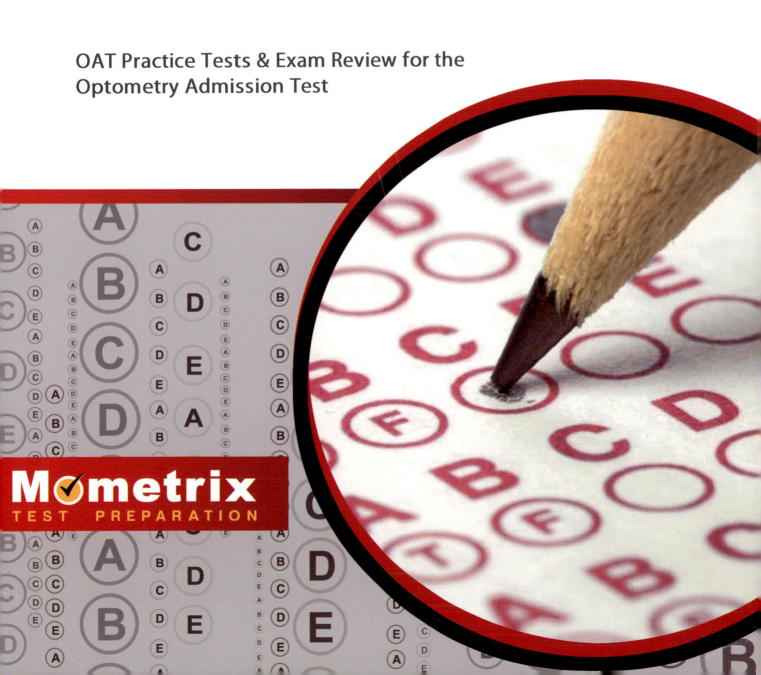

Table of Contents

Practice Test 1

Natural Science

Biology

1. The breakdown of a disaccharide releases energy which is stored as ATP. This is an example of a(n)
   a. Combination reaction
   b. Replacement reaction
   c. Endothermic reaction
   d. Exothermic reaction
   e. Thermodynamic reaction

2. Which of the following molecules is thought to have acted as the first enzyme in early life on earth?
   a. Protein
   b. RNA
   c. DNA
   d. Triglycerides
   e. Phospholipids

3. Cyanide is a poison that binds to the active site of the enzyme cytochrome c and prevents its activity. Cyanide is a(n)
   a. Prosthetic group
   b. Cofactor
   c. Coenzyme
   d. Inhibitor
   e. Reverse regulator

4. In photosynthesis, high-energy electrons move through electron transport chains to produce ATP and NADPH. Which of the following provides the energy to create high energy electrons?
   a. NADH
   b. NADP+
   c. O2
   d. Water
   e. Light

5. The synaptonemal complex is present in which of the following phases of the cell cycle?
   a. Metaphase of mitosis
   b. Metaphase of meiosis I
   c. Telophase of meiosis I
   d. Metaphase of meiosis II
   e. Telophase of meiosis II

6. Which type of plant has leaves with parallel veins?
   a. Monocots
   b. Dicots
   c. Angiosperms
   d. Gymnosperms
   e. Nonvascular plants

7. In ferns, the joining of egg and sperm produces a zygote, which will grow into the
   a. Gametophyte
   b. Sporophyte
   c. Spore
   d. Sporangium
   e. Seedling

Questions 8 and 9 pertain to the following diagram of a complete, perfect flower

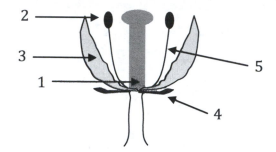

8. The structure in which microspores are produced.
   a. 1
   b. 2
   c. 3
   d. 4
   e. 5

9. The structures composed solely of diploid cells
   a. 1, 2, and 3
   b. 2, 3, and 4
   c. 3, 4, and 5
   d. 1, 4, and 5
   e. 1, 2, and 4

10. Which of the following processes is an example of positive feedback?
    a. High CO2 blood levels stimulate respiration which decreases blood CO2 levels
    b. High blood glucose levels stimulate insulin release, which makes muscle and liver cells take in glucose
    c. Increased nursing stimulates increased milk production in mammary glands
    d. Low blood oxygen levels stimulate erythropoietin production which increases red blood cell production by bone marrow
    e. Low blood calcium levels stimulate parathyroid hormone release from the parathyroid gland. Parathyroid hormone stimulates calcium release from bones.

11. In which of the following stages of embryo development are the three primary germ layers first present?
    a. Zygote
    b. Gastrula
    c. Morula
    d. Blastula
    e. Coelomate

12. In the food chain below, vultures represent
    grass → cow → wolf → vulture

    a. Scavengers
    b. Detritivores
    c. Primary carnivores
    d. Herbivores
    e. Secondary consumers

13. A population of 1000 individuals has 110 births and 10 deaths in a year. Its growth rate (r) is equal to
    a. 0.01 per year
    b. 0.1 per year
    c. 0.09 per year
    d. 0.11 per year
    e. 0.009 per year

14. When a population reaches its carrying capacity
    a. Other populations will be forced out of the habitat
    b. Density-dependent factors no longer play a role
    c. Density-independent factors no longer play a role
    d. The population growth rate approaches zero
    e. The population size begins to decrease

15. Darwin's idea that evolution occurs by the gradual accumulation of small changes can be summarized as
   a. Punctuated equilibrium
   b. Phyletic gradualism
   c. Convergent evolution
   d. Adaptive radiation
   e. Sympatric speciation

16. Human predation has cause the population of cheetahs to decline dramatically. Changes in allele frequencies in the remaining population of cheetahs would most likely be due to
   a. Mutation
   b. The bottleneck effect
   c. The founder effect
   d. Gene flow
   e. Natural selection

17. Which of the following carbohydrate polymers serves as an energy storage molecule in plants?
   a. Chitin
   b. Cellulose
   c. Starch
   d. Glycogen
   e. Phospholipids

18. All of the following molecules are soluble in water except:
   a. Polysaccharides
   b. Hydroxyl groups
   c. Carboxylic acids
   d. Polypeptides
   e. Triglycerides

19. The diagram below depicts a metabolic pathway. When product D accumulates, the production of product C decreases, D is an inhibitor of which enzyme?

$$A \xrightarrow{A'} B \xrightarrow{B'} C \longrightarrow \begin{array}{c} D \xrightarrow{D'} E \xrightarrow{E'} F \\ \searrow \\ G \end{array}$$

   a. A′
   b. B′
   c. C′
   d. D′
   e. E′

20. Which of the following is a characteristic of an enzyme cofactor?
   a. It binds to an enzyme's active site
   b. It is consumed in the enzymatic reaction
   c. It inhibits the enzymatic reaction
   d. It binds to an allosteric site
   e. It is covalently bound to the enzyme

21. In photosynthesis, high-energy electrons in Photosystem II are transferred along an electron transport chain and eventually end up in high-energy molecules used in the Calvin Cycle. Which molecule provides electrons to replace those lost by Photosystem II after light stimulation?
   a. NADPH
   b. H2O
   c. ATP
   d. CO2
   e. FADH2

22. Auxin stimulates stem elongation and is involved in the process of phototropism. If plants bend toward a light source, in which region of the plant is auxin most likely to be found?
   a. The sunny side of a stem
   b. The shaded side of a stem
   c. The top of a shoot
   d. The bottom of a shoot
   e. The top side of leaves

23. Which of the following organisms has a circulatory system in which blood circulates in an internal cavity called a hemocoel?
   a. Earthworms
   b. Cats
   c. Birds
   d. Centipedes
   e. Eels

24. In animals, consuming glucose causes insulin release from the pancreas, which causes the liver and muscles to take in glucose from the blood stream. This is an example of:
   a. Thermoregulation
   b. Circulatory feedback
   c. Positive feedback
   d. Negative feedback
   e. Receptor feedback

25. What will be the genotype of the gametes produced by a *Tt* individual?
    a. All T
    b. All t
    c. ½ T and ½ t
    d. All Tt
    e. ½ Tt and ½ *tT*

26. Hemophilia is a sex-linked trait. From which parent(s) did an affected boy inherit the trait?
    a. Only the father
    b. Only the mother
    c. Both the father and the mother
    d. The mother or the father but not both
    e. Impossible to tell

27. Which of the following is the major way in which nitrogen is assimilated into living things?
    a. Erosion from sediments
    b. Fixation by bacteria
    c. Respiration from the atmosphere
    d. Transpiration
    e. Absorption from soils

28. If a population's growth rate is zero, it has likely reached its
    a. Minimal viable population size
    b. Full range
    c. Carrying capacity
    d. Mature age structure
    e. Intrinsic growth rate

29. As a result of herbicide treatment, nearly an entire population of a grass possesses an herbicide-resistant gene. This is an example of:
    a. Stabilizing selection
    b. Directional selection
    c. Disruptive selection
    d. Sexual selection
    e. Artificial selection

30. A population of pea plants has 25% dwarf plants and 75% tall plants. The tall allele, *T*, is dominant to dwarf (*t*). What percentage of tall plants is heterozygous?
    a. 0.75
    b. 0.67
    c. 0.5
    d. 0.25
    e. 0.16

- 8 -

31. The absence of which of the following molecules in the earth's early atmosphere allowed chemical evolution to occur?
    a. CO_2
    b. O_2
    c. H_2
    d. HCl
    e. S

32. Which of the following is not a characteristic of enzymes?
    a. They change shape when they bind their substrates
    b. They can catalyze reactions in both forward and reverse directions
    c. Their activity is sensitive to changes in temperature
    d. They are always active on more than one kind of substrate
    e. They may have more than one binding site

33. In DNA replication, which of the following enzymes is required for separating the DNA molecule into two strands?
    a. DNA polymerase
    b. Single strand binding protein
    c. DNA gyrase
    d. Helicase
    e. Primase

34. Substrate for DNA ligase
    a. Okazaki fragments
    b. RNA primer
    c. Single-strand binding protein
    d. Leading strand
    e. Replication fork

35. Which of the following could be an end product of transcription?
    a. rRNA
    b. DNA
    c. Protein
    d. snRNP
    e. Amino acids

36. Which of the following would be the most likely means of thermoregulation for a mammal in a cold environment?
    a. Adjusting body surface area
    b. Sweating
    c. Countercurrent exchange
    d. Muscle contractions
    e. Increased blood flow to extremities

37. Spermatogenesis occurs in the
    a. Prostate gland
    b. Vas deferens
    c. Seminal vesicles
    d. Penis
    e. Seminiferous tubules

38. Red-green color blindness is an X-linked trait. What is the probability that a mother that is heterozygous for this trait and a father with this trait will have affected children?
    a. 0
    b. ¼
    c. ½
    d. ¾
    e. 1

39. In humans, more than one gene contributes to the trait of hair color. This is an example of
    a. Pleiotropy
    b. Polygenic inheritance
    c. Codominance
    d. Linkage
    e. Epistasis

40. A child is born with type A blood and his mother has type A. Which of the following is NOT a possible combination of genotypes for the mother and father?
    a. IAIB and ii
    b. IAi and ii
    c. IA i and IB i
    d. IAi and IBIB
    e. IAIB and IBi

General Chemistry

1. Which of the following tend to increase the melting point of a solid?
    I. Increasing molecular weight
    II. Decreasing polarity
    III. Increasing surface area
    a. I and II
    b. II
    c. III
    d. I and III

2. One mole of oxygen gas and two moles of hydrogen are combined in a sealed container at STP. Which of the following statements is true?
   a. The mass of hydrogen gas is greater than the mass of oxygen.
   b. The volume of hydrogen is greater than the volume of oxygen.
   c. The hydrogen and oxygen will react to produce 2 mol of water.
   d. The partial pressure of hydrogen is greater than the partial pressure of oxygen.

3. One mole of an ideal gas is compressed to 10 L and heated to 25 °C. What is the pressure of the gas?
   a. 2.4 KPa
   b. 2.4 atm
   c. 0.2 atm
   d. 0.2 KPa

4. Which of the following statements is true about the physical properties of liquids and gases?
      I. Liquids and gases are both compressible
      II. Liquids flow, but gases do not
      III. Liquids flow, and gases are incompressible
      IV. Liquids flow and gases are compressible
      V. Gases flow and liquids are incompressible
   a. I and III
   b. II and IV
   c. III and V
   d. IV and V

5. 1 mole of water and 1 mole of argon are in a cylinder at 110 °C and 1 atm of pressure. The temperature of the cylinder is reduced to -5 °C. Which statement about the contents of the cylinder is most accurate?
   a. The pressure in the cylinder is decreased, and the partial pressure of argon is less than that of water.
   b. The pressure in the cylinder is about the same, and the partial pressure of water is less than that of argon.
   c. The pressure in the cylinder is decreased, and the partial pressure of water is much less than that of argon.
   d. The pressure in the cylinder is decreased and the partial pressure of water is the same as argon.

6. Silver nitrate ($AgNO_3$) is dissolved in water. One drop of an aqueous solution containing NaCl is added and almost instantly, a white milky precipitate forms. What is the precipitate?
   a. NaCl
   b. $NaNO_3$
   c. $AgNO_3$
   d. AgCl

7. Comparing pure water and a 1 M aqueous solution of NaCl, both at 1 atm of pressure, which of the following statements is most accurate?
   a. The pure water will boil at a higher temperature, and be less conductive
   b. The pure water will boil at a lower temperature and be less conductive
   c. The pure water will boil at a lower temperature and be more conductive
   d. The pure water boil at the same temperature and be more conductive

8. 50 grams of acetic acid $C_2H_4O_2$ are dissolved in 200 g of water. Calculate the weight % and mole fraction of the acetic acid in the solution.
   a. 20%, 0.069
   b. 0.069%, 0.20
   c. 25%, 0.075
   d. 20%, 0.075

9. One liter of a 0.02 M solution of methanol in water is prepared. What is the mass of methanol in the solution, and what is the approximate molality of methanol?
   a. 0.64 g, 0.02 m
   b. 0.32 g, 0.01 m
   c. 0.64 g, 0.03 m
   d. 0.32 g, 0.02 m

10. A material has a half life of 2 years. If you started with 1 kg of the material, how much would be left after 8 years?
   a. 1 kg
   b. 0.5 kg
   c. 0.06 kg
   d. 0.12 kg

11. Which of the following statements about radioactive decay is true?
   a. The sum of the mass of the daughter particles is less than that of the parent nucleus
   b. The sum of the mass of the daughter particles is greater than that of the parent nucleus
   c. The sum of the mass of the daughter particles is equal to that of the parent nucleus
   d. The sum of the mass of the daughter particles cannot be accurately measured

12. Hund's rule regarding electronic configuration states:
   a. Electrons in the same orbital must have an opposite spin
   b. Electrons must fill lower energy orbitals before filling higher energy orbitals
   c. Electrons must populate empty orbitals of equal energy before filling occupied orbitals
   d. Electrons must have the same nuclear spin as the nucleus

13. Arrange the following compounds from most polar to least polar:

F_2, CH_3CH_2Cl, $NaCl$, CH_3OH

    a. $NaCl > CH_3OH > CH_3CH_2Cl > F_2$

    b. $F_2 > NaCl > CH_3OH > CH_3CH_2Cl$

    c. $CH_3OH > NaCl > F_2 > CH_3CH_2Cl$

    d. $NaCl > F_2 > CH_3OH > CH_3CH_2Cl$

14. What is the chemical composition of ammonium sulfate?

    a. N 21%, H 3%, S 24%, O 32%

    b. N 10%, H 6%, S 24%, O 60%

    c. N 10%, H 4%, S 12%, O 74%

    d. N 21%, H 6%, S 24%, O 48%

15. Calculate the mass of water produced from the reaction of 1 kg of n-heptane with oxygen.

n-heptane (1 kg) + 11 O_2 → 7 CO_2 + 8 H_2O

    a. 144 g

    b. 8 kg

    c. 800 g

    d. 1.4 kg

16. The overall reaction A→D can be described by the following equation:

A $\xrightarrow{\text{fast}}$ B $\xrightarrow{\text{slow}}$ C $\xrightarrow{\text{fast}}$ D

What would be the rate law for the overall reaction of A to D?

    a. Rate = k[D]/[A]

    b. Rate = k[B]

    c. Rate = [B]

    d. Rate = k[C]/[B]

17. Which of the following are considered Lewis acids?

    I. H_2SO_4

    II. $AlCl_3$

    III. PCl_3

    IV. $FeCl_3$

    a. II and IV

    b. II and III

    c. I and IV

    d. I and II

18. What is the pH of a buffer containing 0.2 M NaOAc and 0.1 M AcOH? The pka of acetic acid is 4.75.

    a. 4

    b. 5

    c. 6

    d. 7

19. 100 g of NH_3 are cooled from 100 °C to 25 °C. What is the heat change for this transition? The heat capacity of ammonia gas is 35.1 J/(mol) (°K)
   a. -263KJ
   b. 15.5 KJ
   c. -15.5KJ
   d. 263 KJ

20. Which of the following molecules are alkenes?

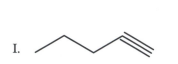

   a. I
   b. II
   c. III
   d. IV

21. Methyl mercury is a toxin produced indirectly from what energy source?
   a. Oil
   b. Natural gas
   c. Wood
   d. Coal

22. A liquid is heated from 50 °C to 80 °C. Which of the following statements is generally true about the solubility of solids and gases in the liquid?
   a. The solubility of solids will increase and the solubility of gases will decrease
   b. The solubility of solids will decrease and the solubility of gases will increase
   c. The solubility of solids will increase and the solubility of gases will increase
   d. The solubility of solids will decrease and the solubility of gases will decrease

23. Adding a catalyst to a reaction will do which of the following to that reaction:
   a. Shift the reaction equilibrium towards the products
   b. Increase the temperature of the reaction
   c. Decrease the energy of activation for the reaction
   d. Increase the purity of the reaction products

24. Place the following in the correct order of increasing acidity:
H_3PO_4, HF, HCl, H_2O, NH_3
    a. $H_3PO4<H_2O<NH_3<HF<HCl$
    b. $NH_3<H_2O<HF<H_3PO_4<HCl$
    c. $H_2O<NH_3<HF<H_3PO_4<HCl$
    d. $NH_3<H_2O<HF<HCl<H_3PO_4$

25. To make a good buffering system in the pH range of 5-9, which acid/base combinations would likely work the best?
    a. HCl/NaOH
    b. $HNO_3/NaNO_3$
    c. $H_2SO_4/NaHSO_4$
    d. NaH_2PO_4/Na_2HPO_4

26. Determine the heat of combustion for the following reaction:
Propane + 5 O_2 → 3 CO_2 + 4 H_2O
The standard heats of formation for propane, CO_2 and water are -103.8 KJ/mol, -393.5 KJ/mol and -285.8 KJ/mol respectively.
    a. -2220 KJ/mol
    b. -2323.7 kJ/mol
    c. 2220 KJ/mol
    d. 2323.7 KJ/mol

27. A 1kg block each of iron, lead and nickel are heated from 20 °C to 30 °C. Which of the following statements about the blocks is true?
    a. The lead will heat faster than the iron and the nickel.
    b. The iron required more heat to reach 30 °C than the nickel or lead.
    c. All three blocks required a different amount of heat to reach 30 °C.
    d. The iron required more time to reach 30 °C.

28. In the reaction Pb + H_2SO_4 +H_2O →$PbSO_4$ +H_2 +H_2O
    a. Lead is reduced and hydrogen is oxidized
    b. Lead is oxidized and hydrogen is oxidized
    c. Lead is reduced and sulfate is oxidized
    d. Lead is oxidized and hydrogen is reduced

29. Which of the following elements would likely be good reducing agents?
    a. Br_2
    b. N_2
    c. Na
    d. Ne

30. Molten magnesium chloride is electrolyzed. The products formed from this reaction are:
    a. $Mg(0)$ at the anode and $Cl-$ at the cathode
    b. $Mg2+$ at the anode and $Cl-$ at the cathode
    c. $Mg (0)$ at the cathode and Cl_2 at the anode
    d. $Mg(0)$ at the anode and Cl_2 at the cathode

Organic Chemistry

1. The general formula for an alkane is
    a. C_nH_{2n}
    b. C_nH_{2n+2}
    c. $C_{2n}H_{2n+2}$
    d. $(CH_2)_n$

2. An unknown substance is found to have a sharp melting point, and therefore
    a. it is a pure compound
    b. it may be a pure compound
    c. it may be a eutectic mixture of compounds
    d. both b) and c) are true

3. The sp^3 orbital is a hybrid of
    a. three sp orbitals
    b. the $3s$ and a $3p$ orbital
    c. the s and three p orbitals of the same principal quantum level
    d. three p orbitals of one principal quantum level and the s orbital of the next

4. Propanol, propanal and propanone
    a. have equal molecular weights
    b. are not reactive compounds
    c. have a three-carbon molecular backbone
    d. none of the above

5. Carboxylic acids (R-COOH) and alcohols (R'-OH) undergo a condensation reaction to form
    a. esters and water
    b. ethers and water
    c. a diacid
    d. a lactone

6. When two high priority substituent groups are restricted to opposite sides of a molecule they are designated as
   a. Z- isomers
   b. E- isomers
   c. R- isomers
   d. d,l- isomers

7. An sp^2 carbon atom that can form an asymmetric sp^3 carbon atom is called
   a. prochiral
   b. delocalized
   c. stabilized
   d. a resonance structure

8. A molecule with two adjacent chiral centers that are enantiomeric is called
   a. a *meso-* structure
   b. a *d,l-* pair
   c. a racemate
   d. a lone pair

9. The carbonyl group is found
   a. only in ketones and carboxylic acid derivatives
   b. only in ketones and aldehydes
   c. only in aldehydes and amides
   d. in aldehydes, ketones, and carboxylic acid derivatives

10. The NMR spectrum of a compound shows a triplet near $\delta1.0$ and a related quartet near $\delta1.3$ with the integration ratio of 3:2. This indicates
   a. an isopropyl group is present in the molecule
   b. an ethyl group is present in the molecule
   c. the compound is an ethyl ester
   d. one or more identical ethyl groups are present in the molecule

11. Carbon-carbon double bonds can be converted to vicinal diols by reaction with
   a. $KMnO_4$ in cold methanol
   b. $KMnO_4$ in hot acid solution
   c. $KMnO_4$ in cold methanolic KOH solution
   d. $K_2Cr_2O_7$ in cold methanolic KOH solution

12. Colored impurities can often be removed from a compound during the recrystallization process by
   a. filtration
   b. addition of a cosolvent
   c. addition of activated charcoal powder
   d. chromatography

13. Which of the following pairs of compounds are carbohydrates?
    a. glucose and cellulose
    b. starch and caffeine
    c. levulose and gallic acid
    d. mannose and pyridine

14. A carbonyl compound with α protons can undergo
    a. racemization
    b. inversion
    c. keto-enol tautomerism
    d. conformational isomerism

15. A Friedel-Crafts reaction requires the presence of
    a. HCl and Cl_2
    b. $AlCl_3$ or $FeCl_3$
    c. a Lewis base
    d. benzene

16. The reaction of benzene with excess benzyl bromide and $AlCl_3$ produces
    a. diphenyl methane
    b. no reaction
    c. 1,2-diphenylethane
    d. biphenyl

17. Amides can be produced by reaction of acyl halides with
    a. 1º and 2º amines
    b. 1º and 3º amines
    c. 2º and 3º amines
    d. 1º, 2º and 3º amines

18. Phosphorus has typical oxidation states of
    a. -3 and -5
    b. +2 and +6
    c. +3 and +5
    d. +3 and -3

19. When a solution of 4-t-butylcyclohexanone is treated with two equivalents of a strong base, followed by addition of a two-fold excess of 1-bromobutane, then quenched with water the product is
    a. 2-butyl-4-t-butylcyclohexanone
    b. 2-butyl-4-t-butylcyclohexanol
    c. 2,6-dibutyl-4-t-butylcyclohexanone
    d. 2,6-dibutyl-4-t-butylcyclohexanol

20. The primary structure of a protein molecule is determined by
    a. the relative positions of amino acid residues according to bond angles
    b. the sequential order of amino acid residues in the molecule
    c. the folding of the molecule at specific amino acid residues in the molecular structure
    d. the geometry of cavities in the overall molecular structure

21. Birch reduction employs
    a. activated charcoal powder from birch wood
    b. sodium amide
    c. sodium metal dissolved in liquid ammonia
    d. sodium metal in refluxing THF

22. An S_N2 reaction mechanism results in
    a. formation of a carbonium ion intermediate
    b. inversion of stereochemistry at the site of reaction
    c. formation of alcohols
    d. formation of carbon-carbon double bonds

23. Alcohols and amines react with p-toluenesulfonyl chloride to produce
    a. tosylates
    b. tosylates and tosylamides
    c. tosylamino alcohols
    d. tosyl chlorides

24. A condensation reaction between two carboxylic acid molecules produces
    a. acetic anhydride
    b. a mixed anhydride
    c. an anhydride and water
    d. maleic anhydride

25. Separation of compounds by distillation is more efficient when
    a. carried out under reduced pressure
    b. more condensation-vaporization cycles occur
    c. carried out quickly
    d. the condenser is very cold

26. A six-carbon sugar whose acyclic form is an aldehyde is called
    a. a pentohexose
    b. a lactose
    c. an aldohexose
    d. a ketofuranose

27. A sugar molecule whose acyclic form is a five-membered oxygen-containing heterocyclic ring is called
   a. a pyranose
   b. a furanose
   c. a pentose
   d. a cyclohexose

28. Sucrose ($C_{12}H_{22}O_{11}$), common white sugar, is
a. a disaccharide of glucose and fructose
b. an oligosaccharide of several small sugar molecules
c. has only four –OH groups
   d. does not dissolve in organic solvents

29. A six-carbon sugar whose acyclic form is a ketone is
   a. unknown
   b. called a ketohexose
   c. a polyhydroxy enone
   d. called an aldopentose

30. Compounds that have atoms other than carbon in their ring structures are called
   a. carbocycles
   b. paracycles
   c. macrocycles
   d. heterocycles

Reading Comprehension

Questions 1 – 9 are based on the following passage:

On a bad day, have you ever been irritable? Have you ever used a harsh tone or even been verbally disrespectful to your parents or teachers? Everyone has a short temper from time to time, but current statistics indicate that between 16% and 20% of a school's population suffer from a psychological condition known as <u>Oppositional</u> Defiance Disorder, or ODD.

ODD symptoms include difficulty complying with adult requests, excessive arguments with adults, temper tantrums, difficulty accepting responsibility for actions, <u>low frustration tolerance</u>, and behaviors intended to annoy or upset adults. Parents of children with ODD can often feel as though their whole relationship is based on conflict after conflict.

Unfortunately, ODD can be caused by a number of factors. Some students affected by ODD suffer abuse, neglect, and severe or unpredictable discipline at home. Others have parents with mood disorders or have experienced family violence. Various types of therapy are helpful in treating ODD, and some drugs can treat particular symptoms. However, no single cure exists.

The best advice from professionals is directed toward parents. Therapists encourage parents to avoid situations that usually end in power struggles, to try not to <u>feed into</u> oppositional behavior by reacting emotionally, to praise positive behaviors, and to discourage negative behaviors with timeouts instead of harsh discipline.

1. Which of the following statements can be inferred from paragraph 4?
   a. Parents of children with ODD are bad parents.
   b. ODD is not a real psychological disorder.
   c. Medication can worsen ODD.
   d. Reacting emotionally to defiant behavior might worsen the behavior.

2. Which of the following best describes the main idea of this passage?
   a. ODD has no cause.
   b. ODD is a complex condition.
   c. Parents with ODD should seek support.
   d. Parents are the cause of ODD.

3. As used in this passage, the word <u>oppositional</u> most nearly means:
   a. Uncooperative
   b. Violent
   c. Passive aggressive
   d. Altruistic

4. Which of the following can be inferred from paragraph one?
    a. Most children who speak harshly to their parents have ODD.
    b. Most people exhibit symptoms of ODD occasionally.
    c. Between 16% and 20% of the school population has been abused.
    d. A short temper is a symptom of obsessive compulsive disorder.

5. As used in this passage, the phrase <u>feed into</u> most nearly means:
    a. Discourage
    b. Ignore
    c. Encourage
    d. Abuse

6. As used in this passage, the phrase <u>low frustration tolerance</u> most nearly means:
    a. Patience
    b. Low IQ
    c. Difficulty dealing with frustration
    d. The ability to cope with frustration

7. The author's purpose in writing this passage is to:
    a. Express frustration about ODD.
    b. Prove that parents are the cause of ODD.
    c. Inform the reader about this complex condition.
    d. Persuade the reader to keep students with ODD out of public school.

8. According to the passage, which of the following is a cause of ODD?
    a. Excessive television viewing.
    b. Poor diet.
    c. Severe or unpredictable punishment.
    d. Low IQ.

9. Based on the passage, which of the following statements seems most true?
    a. A variety of parenting techniques can be used to help children with ODD.
    b. Children with ODD must be physically aggressive to be diagnosed.
    c. Parents of children with ODD often engage in risk-taking activities.
    d. Harsh disciplinary measures must be used to control children with ODD.

Questions 10 – 17 are based on the following passage:

Plastics have long been considered one of the great conveniences of the modern era, but evidence is mounting to indicate that these conveniences have come at an incredible cost. The <u>chief</u> benefit of plastics is their <u>durability</u>, but this benefit turns out to be the same reason plastic has become a significant problem: It takes between *two and four hundred years* to decompose. All of this plastic has accumulated into a catastrophic mess and has also caused disease in humans.

Between Hawaii and Japan, a giant mass of plastic twice the size of Texas slowly swirls with the currents of the Pacific Ocean. This area has come to be known as the Great Pacific Garbage Patch, and its effects on the ecology of the ocean are unimaginable. According to United Nations researchers, a hundred thousand sea mammals and a million seabirds die each year. They are found with cigarette lighters, syringes, and other plastics that they mistake for food in their stomachs.

Evidence also indicates that the plastic we store our food in poses health risks. For instance, phthalates (pronounced "THEY-lates") have been shown to have detrimental effects on the reproductive system, yet they are found in many plastic products—including baby bottles and water bottles. They have also been linked to various forms of cancer. Additionally, a chemical called bisphenol A that is found in many plastics can <u>mimic</u> the effects of the hormone estrogen, which can also affect the reproductive system.

In short, plastics may turn out to be a lot less convenient than they seem!

10. Which of the following best describes the author's purpose in writing this passage?
    a. To persuade readers to accept the author's point of view.
    b. To explain the benefits of plastic.
    c. To explain the risks of plastic bottles.
    d. To inform the reader of the effects of phthalates in plastics.

11. As used in this passage, the word "chief" most nearly means:
    a. Main
    b. Least likely
    c. Benefit
    d. Leader of a Native American tribe

12. Which of the following statements can be inferred from paragraph two?
    a. The Great Pacific Garbage Patch is not a significant threat to humans.
    b. No one has determined why sea mammals and seabirds are dying at an alarming rate.
    c. The Great Pacific Garbage Patch is too large to be cleaned up by one country.
    d. Ocean currents carry the plastic to the middle of the ocean.

13. Which of the following statements best summarizes the main idea of this passage?
    a. The benefits of plastics outweigh their risks.
    b. Plastics pose a significant threat to humans and other living creatures.
    c. Phthalates should not be used in baby bottles.
    d. Plastics decompose very slowly.

14. As used in this passage, the word "mimic" most nearly means:
    a. Reduce
    b. Cancerous
    c. Intensify
    d. Resemble

15. What particular risk does the author say the Great Pacific Garbage Patch poses to marine animals?
    a. It affects yearly temperature averages.
    b. Animals accidentally ingest the plastics and die.
    c. The animals' habitat is poisoned by phthalates.
    d. Seabirds cannot get to the fish below the garbage.

16. Why does this passage not discuss more of plastics' benefits?
    a. Plastics have no benefits.
    b. The passage emphasizes the dangers over the benefits in order to prove that plastics are harmful.
    c. The passage devotes a significant amount of attention to the benefits of plastics.
    d. Discussing the benefits would contradict the author's point that plastics are a necessary evil.

17. According to the passage, the word "durability" most nearly means:
    a. Decomposition
    b. Permanence
    c. Coloration
    d. Poisonous

Questions 18 – 24 are based on the follow paragraph:

Living things such as animals and plants consist of immense clusters of atoms organized into compartments called cells. A man consists of nearly ten octillion (ten followed by 27 zeros) atoms. This huge collection of atoms is capable of consciousness, joy and suffering, the ability to distinguish between good and evil, and many other complex emotional behaviors. The organism itself is characterized by an almost limitless variety of traits. Most remarkably, all living things are formed in a manner that allows them to survive and to reproduce in some existing environment.

There are two schools of thought that seek to explain this remarkable habituation of organisms and their environments. Transcendentalists invoke preternatural forces, to which they assign responsibility for the design of complex organisms that are uniquely adapted to equally complex environments. Mechanists, in contrast, submit that life can be understood without recourse to such forces. They hold that complex biological structures are simply highly evolved chemical or physical phenomena. The foremost proponent of the mechanist viewpoint was Darwin, who painted a picture of the evolution of modern organisms through gradual changes between ancestors and offspring, changes that took place over billions of years of evolutionary history.

Darwin posited natural selection as the driving mechanism for these changes. Natural selection is the differential reproduction of organisms that are more or less adapted to the environments they inhabit. It is strictly a biological phenomenon, since it depends upon reproduction. It requires a mechanism for the generation of diversity, which is provided by the molecular process of mutation. In addition, it requires that selected traits be heritable. In the years since it was first described, natural selection has been successful in explaining an enormous catalog of biological observations and has become one of the fundamental pillars of modern biology.

Although Darwin is its best-known proponent, the mechanist school of thought has its roots in the earlier work of the seventeenth century scholar René Descartes, the same man who gave us the Cartesian coordinate system used in mathematics. The Cartesian approach to biology was a strictly reductionist one that sought to describe life completely in terms of the chemical and physical processes that make up living organisms. Ultimately, this approach would reduce all of biology to the status of a specialized branch of chemistry. And it must be said, there have been some outstanding successes based upon this approach. The elucidation of the role of nucleic acids in the transmission of hereditary traits is a prime example.

Many molecular biologists have come to believe that once the study of biological chemistry has progressed sufficiently, even the most complex biological phenomena will be able to be predicted based upon simple physicochemical interactions. But while the importance of molecular biology is beyond argument today, there are those who doubt that all of biology can be deduced from simple laws of chemistry and physics. Such doubts need not have recourse to transcendental explanations, but point instead to the increasing complexity of biological organization. The biosphere is organized into a hierarchy of levels: molecular, cellular, organismic, populational, ecosystemic. Each of these levels is characterized by laws and principles of its own. Thus, the psychological axioms that govern the interactions of living things at the levels of organisms and populations are simply not relevant to the laws of chemistry, which describe the molecular and cellular levels. In this view, while simple chemical principles may underlie all of biology, they are insufficient to explain the interactions that take place at higher levels. In a sense, the laws that govern biology have evolved, as well as the organisms and systems that they describe.

18. The organism referred to is
   a. Man
   b. Any huge collection of atoms
   c. Any living collection of atoms
   d. Things capable of distinguishing between good and evil
   e. Living things made of ten octillion atoms

19. Which pairing best represents the two schools of thought described in the second paragraph of the text?
    a. Large and small
    b. Moral and amoral
    c. Complex and simple
    d. Theoretical and practical
    e. Supernatural and chemical

20. The best synonym for the word "posit" used in the passage is
    a. Position
    b. Postulate
    c. Assume
    d. Claim
    e. Reject

21. The purpose of the third paragraph is to
    a. Prove that evolution is correct
    b. Describe a process that is necessary for the theory of evolution to be correct
    c. Discuss biology and reproduction
    d. Repeat some things that Darwin said
    e. Refute claims made by transcendentalists

22. According to the text, René Descartes was
    a. The first mechanist
    b. The foremost mechanist
    c. A chemist
    d. A reductionist
    e. A teacher

23. A strict reductionist would believe that
    a. Psychological axioms can be explained by chemistry and physics
    b. Ecosystems are characterized by laws and principles of their own
    c. Transcendental explanations are required to understand psychology
    d. Living organisms are made up of physical processes
    e. Darwin and Descartes worked together

24. The overall purpose of the passage is best described as
    a. A defense of Darwin's theory
    b. Drawing a contrast between Darwin and Descartes
    c. A description of the role of mathematics in biology
    d. Showing the context of evolutionary theory in biology
    e. Showing the limits of natural selection

Questions 25 – 28 are based on the following passage:

Foodborne illnesses are contracted by eating food or drinking beverages contaminated with bacteria, parasites, or viruses. Harmful chemicals can also cause foodborne illnesses if they have contaminated food during harvesting or processing. Foodborne illnesses can cause symptoms ranging from upset stomach to diarrhea, fever, vomiting, abdominal cramps, and dehydration. Most foodborne infections are undiagnosed and unreported, though the Centers for Disease Control and Prevention estimates that every year about 76 million people in the United States become ill from pathogens in food. About 5,000 of these people die.

Harmful bacteria are the most common cause of foodborne illness. Some bacteria may be present at the point of purchase. Raw foods are the most common source of foodborne illnesses because they are not sterile; examples include raw meat and poultry contaminated during slaughter. Seafood may become contaminated during harvest or processing. One in 10,000 eggs may be contaminated with Salmonella inside the shell. Produce, such as spinach, lettuce, tomatoes, sprouts, and melons, can become contaminated with Salmonella, Shigella, or Escherichia coli (E. coli). Contamination can occur during growing, harvesting, processing, storing, shipping, or final preparation. Sources of produce contamination vary, as these foods are grown in soil and can become contaminated during growth, processing, or distribution. Contamination may also occur during food preparation in a restaurant or a home kitchen. The most common form of contamination from handled foods is the calicivirus, also called the Norwalk-like virus.

When food is cooked and left out for more than two hours at room temperature, bacteria can multiply quickly. Most bacteria don't produce an odor or change in color or texture, so they can be impossible to detect. Freezing food slows or stops bacteria's growth, but does not destroy the bacteria. The microbes can become reactivated when the food is thawed. Refrigeration also can slow the growth of some bacteria. Thorough cooking is required to destroy the bacteria.

25. What is the subject of the passage?
    a. foodborne illnesses
    b. the dangers of uncooked food
    c. bacteria
    d. proper food preparation

26. Which statement is *not* a detail from the passage?
    a. Every year, more than 70 million Americans contract some form of foodborne illness.
    b. Once food is cooked, it cannot cause illness.
    c. Refrigeration can slow the growth of some bacteria.
    d. The most common form of contamination in handled foods is calicivirus.

27. What is the meaning of the word *pathogens* as it is used in the first paragraph?
    a. diseases
    b. vaccines
    c. disease-causing substances
    d. foods

28. What is the meaning of the word *sterile* as it is used in the second paragraph?
    a. free of bacteria
    b. healthy
    c. delicious
    d. impotent

Questions 29 – 32 are based on the following passage:

There are a number of health problems related to bleeding in the esophagus and stomach. Stomach acid can cause inflammation and bleeding at the lower end of the esophagus. This condition, usually associated with the symptom of heartburn, is called esophagitis, or inflammation of the esophagus. Sometimes a muscle between the esophagus and stomach fails to close properly and allows the return of food and stomach juices into the esophagus, which can lead to esophagitis. In another unrelated condition, enlarged veins (varices) at the lower end of the esophagus rupture and bleed massively. Cirrhosis of the liver is the most common cause of esophageal varices. Esophageal bleeding can be caused by a tear in the lining of the esophagus (Mallory-Weiss syndrome). Mallory-Weiss syndrome usually results from vomiting, but may also be caused by increased pressure in the abdomen from coughing, hiatal hernia, or childbirth. Esophageal cancer can cause bleeding.

The stomach is a frequent site of bleeding. Infections with Helicobacter pylori (H. pylori), alcohol, aspirin, aspirin-containing medicines, and various other medicines (such as nonsteroidal anti-inflammatory drugs [NSAIDs]— particularly those used for arthritis) can cause stomach ulcers or inflammation (gastritis). The stomach is often the site of ulcer disease. Acute or chronic ulcers may enlarge and erode through a blood vessel, causing bleeding. Also, patients suffering from burns, shock, head injuries, cancer, or those who have undergone extensive surgery may develop stress ulcers. Bleeding can also occur from benign tumors or cancer of the stomach, although these disorders usually do not cause massive bleeding.

29. What is the main idea of the passage?
    a. The digestive system is complex.
    b. Of all the digestive organs, the stomach is the most prone to bleeding.
    c. Both the esophagus and the stomach are subject to bleeding problems.
    d. Esophagitis afflicts the young and old alike.

30. Which statement is *not* a detail from the passage?
   a. Alcohol can cause stomach bleeding.
   b. Ulcer disease rarely occurs in the stomach.
   c. Benign tumors rarely result in massive bleeding.
   d. Childbirth is one cause of Mallory-Weiss syndrome.

31. What is the meaning of the word *rupture* as it is used in the first paragraph?
   a. tear
   b. collapse
   c. implode
   d. detach

32. What is the meaning of the word *erode* as it is used in the second paragraph?
   a. avoid
   b. divorce
   c. contain
   d. wear away

Questions 33 – 36 are based on the following passage:

We met Kathy Blake while she was taking a stroll in the park . . . by herself. What's so striking about this is that Kathy is completely blind, and she has been for more than 30 years.

The diagnosis from her doctor was retinitis pigmentosa, or RP. It's an incurable genetic disease that leads to progressive visual loss. Photoreceptive cells in the retina slowly start to die, leaving the patient visually impaired.

"Life was great the year before I was diagnosed," Kathy said. "I had just started a new job; I just bought my first new car. I had just started dating my now-husband. Life was good. The doctor had told me that there was some good news and some bad news. 'The bad news is you are going to lose your vision; the good news is we don't think you are going to go totally blind.' Unfortunately, I did lose all my vision within about 15 years."

Two years ago, Kathy got a glimmer of hope. She heard about an artificial retina being developed in Los Angeles. It was experimental, but Kathy was the perfect candidate.

Dr. Mark Humayun is a retinal surgeon and biomedical engineer. "A good candidate for the artificial retina device is a person who is blind because of retinal blindness," he said. "They've lost the rods and cones, the light-sensing cells of the eye, but the rest of the circuitry is relatively intact. In the simplest rendition, this device basically takes a blind person and hooks them up to a camera."

It may sound like the stuff of science fiction . . . and just a few years ago it was. A camera is built into a pair of glasses, sending radio signals to a tiny chip in the back of the retina. The chip, small enough to fit on a fingertip, is implanted surgically and stimulates the nerves that lead to the vision center

- 29 -

of the brain. Kathy is one of twenty patients who have undergone surgery and use the device.

It has been about two years since the surgery, and Kathy still comes in for weekly testing at the University of Southern California's medical campus. She scans back and forth with specially made, camera-equipped glasses until she senses objects on a screen and then touches the objects. The low-resolution image from the camera is still enough to make out the black stripes on the screen. Impulses are sent from the camera to the 60 receptors that are on the chip in her retina. So, what is Kathy seeing?

"I see flashes of light that indicate a contrast from light to dark—very similar to a camera flash, probably not quite as bright because it's not hurting my eye at all," she replied.

Humayun underscored what a breakthrough this is and how a patient adjusts. "If you've been blind for 30 or 50 years, (and) all of a sudden you get this device, there is a period of learning," he said. "Your brain needs to learn. And it's literally like seeing a baby crawl—to a child walk—to an adult run."

While hardly perfect, the device works best in bright light or where there is a lot of contrast. Kathy takes the device home. The software that runs the device can be upgraded. So, as the software is upgraded, her vision improves. Recently, she was outside with her husband on a moonlit night and saw something she hadn't seen for a long time.

"I scanned up in the sky (and) I got a big flash, right where the moon was, and pointed it out. I can't even remember how many years ago it's been that I would have ever been able to do that."

This technology has a bright future. The current chip has a resolution of 60 pixels. Humayun says that number could be increased to more than a thousand in the next version.

"I think it will be extremely exciting if they can recognize their loved ones' faces and be able to see what their wife or husband or their grandchildren look like, which they haven't seen," said Humayun.

Kathy dreams of a day when blindness like hers will be a distant memory. "My eye disease is hereditary," she said. "My three daughters happen to be fine, but I want to know that if my grandchildren ever have a problem, they will have something to give them some vision."

33. What is the primary subject of the passage?
    a. a new artificial retina
    b. Kathy Blake
    c. hereditary disease
    d. Dr. Mark Humayun

34. What is the meaning of the word *progressive* as it is used in the second paragraph?
   a. selective
   b. gradually increasing
   c. diminishing
   d. disabling

35. Which statement is *not* a detail from the passage?
   a. The use of an artificial retina requires a special pair of glasses.
   b. Retinal blindness is the inability to perceive light.
   c. Retinitis pigmentosa is curable.
   d. The artificial retina performs best in bright light.

36. What is the author's intention in writing the essay?
   a. to persuade
   b. to entertain
   c. to analyze
   d. to inform

Questions 37 – 40 are based on the following passage:

The federal government regulates dietary supplements through the United States Food and Drug Administration (FDA). The regulations for dietary supplements are not the same as those for prescription or over-the-counter drugs. In general, the regulations for dietary supplements are less strict.

To begin with, a manufacturer does not have to prove the safety and effectiveness of a dietary supplement before it is marketed. A manufacturer is permitted to say that a dietary supplement addresses a nutrient deficiency, supports health, or is linked to a particular body function (such as immunity), if there is research to support the claim. Such a claim must be followed by the words "This statement has not been evaluated by the Food and Drug Administration. This product is not intended to diagnose, treat, cure, or prevent any disease."

Also, manufacturers are expected to follow certain good manufacturing practices (GMPs) to ensure that dietary supplements are processed consistently and meet quality standards. Requirements for GMPs went into effect in 2008 for large manufacturers and are being phased in for small manufacturers through 2010.

Once a dietary supplement is on the market, the FDA monitors safety and product information, such as label claims and package inserts. If it finds a product to be unsafe, it can take action against the manufacturer and/or distributor and may issue a warning or require that the product be removed from the marketplace. The Federal Trade Commission (FTC) is responsible for regulating product advertising; it requires that all information be truthful and not misleading.

The federal government has taken legal action against a number of dietary supplement promoters or Web sites that promote or sell dietary supplements because they have made false or deceptive statements about their products or because marketed products have proven to be unsafe.

37. What is the main idea of the passage?
    a. Manufacturers of dietary supplements have to follow good manufacturing practices.
    b. The FDA has a special program for regulating dietary supplements.
    c. The federal government prosecutes those who mislead the general public.
    d. The FDA is part of the federal government.

38. Which statement is *not* a detail from the passage?
    a. Promoters of dietary supplements can make any claims that are supported by research.
    b. GMP requirements for large manufacturers went into effect in 2008.
    c. Product advertising is regulated by the FTC.
    d. The FDA does not monitor products after they enter the market.

39. What is the meaning of the phrase *phased in* as it is used in the third paragraph?
    a. stunned into silence
    b. confused
    c. implemented in stages
    d. legalized

40. What is the meaning of the word *deceptive* as it is used in the fifth paragraph?
    a. misleading
    b. malicious
    c. illegal
    d. irritating

Physics

1. The masses of four different objects taken with different scales were 23.04 g, 7.12 g, 0.0088 g and 5.423 g. What is the total mass of all four objects to the proper number of significant digits?
   a. 35.59180
   b. 35.5918
   c. 35.60
   d. 35.59

2. Consider the two vectors below:

Vector A:

Vector B:

Which vector best represents the vector obtained by subtracting A from B ($\vec{B} - \vec{A}$)?

a.    c.

b.    d.

3. You throw a baseball straight up near the surface of Earth and it falls back to the ground. Which statement is true about the acceleration of the baseball at the top of its path? [Ignore air resistance]
   a. The acceleration is zero.
   b. The acceleration changes sign.
   c. The acceleration is -9.8 m/s^2.
   d. The acceleration continues to increase.

4. Consider the following statements about Newton's law:
I. A newton is a fundamental unit.
II. Mass and acceleration are inversely related when the force is constant.
III. Newton's first law can be derived from Newton's second law.
IV. Newton's second law can be derived from the universal law of gravity.
Which of the following statements are true?
   a. I, II, and III.
   b. II and III only.
   c. III only.
   d. I, II, III, and IV are not true.

5. In an amusement park ride, you stand on the floor of a cylindrical ring with your back touching the wall. The ring begins to rotate, slowly at first, but then faster and faster. When the ring is rotating fast enough, the floor is removed. You do not slide down but remained pressed against the wall of the ring. Which is the best explanation for why you don't fall down?
   a. The centripetal force pushes you towards the wall.
   b. The centripetal force changes the direction of your motion.
   c. The force of friction between the wall and your body is greater than your weight.
   d. The rotating ring creates a weightless environment.

6. A 10-kg plastic block is at rest on a flat wooden surface. The coefficient of static friction between wood and plastic is 0.6 and the coefficient of kinetic friction is 0.5. How much horizontal force is needed to start the plastic box moving?
   a. 5 N
   b. 49 N
   c. 59 N
   d. 98 N

7. The pulley in the device below has no mass and is frictionless. The larger mass is 30 kg and the smaller mass is 20 kg. What is the acceleration of the masses?

   a. 0.5 m/s²
   b. 2 m/s²
   c. 9.8 m/s²
   d. 98 m/s²

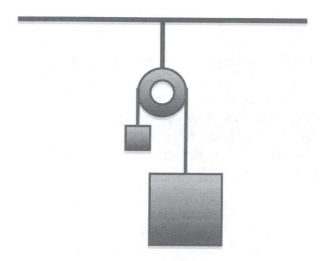

8. Two unequal masses are balanced on a fulcrum using a massless bar, as shown below. If both masses are shifted towards the fulcrum so that their distances from the fulcrum are one-half the original distance, what happens to the masses?

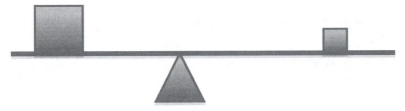

    a. The heavier mass will tilt downward.
    b. The masses will remain balanced.
    c. Cannot be determined from the information given.
    d. The lighter mass will tilt downward.

9. Impulse is measured as the change in an object's momentum. Which statement is correct about the impulse on a ball rolling down a hill? Ignore air resistance and friction.
    a. The impulse is constant.
    b. The impulse only exists for a short time.
    c. The units of impulse are joules per second.
    d. The object's impulse increases.

10. A 75-kg ice skater moving eastward at 5 m/s collides with a 100-kg skater moving northward at 4 m/s. Anticipating the collision, they hug each other and produce an inelastic collision. What is their final speed?
    a. Can't be determined from the information given.
    b. 3.1 m/s
    c. 4.1 m/s
    d. 2.1 m/s

11. Which statement correctly states the work-energy theorem?
    a. The change in kinetic energy of an object is equal to the work done by the object.
    b. The change in kinetic energy of an object is equal to the work done on an object.
    c. The change in potential energy of an object is equal to the work done by the object.
    d. The change in potential energy of an object is equal to the work done on an object.

12. A ball is released from a certain height along a frictionless track that does a loop-the-loop. The loop-the-loop part of the track is a perfect circle of radius R. At what height above the ground must the ball be released from in order to not fall off the track when it gets to the top of the loop-the-loop?
    a. R
    b. $2R$
    c. $\dfrac{5R}{2}$
    d. $3R$

13. Which of the following statements about energy is true?
    a. Mechanical energy is always conserved in an isolated system.
    b. Total energy is always conserved in an isolated system.
    c. Energy is never created or destroyed.
    d. You can determine the mechanical energy of an object by using $E = mc^2$

14. Which of the following statements best explains what is meant by the phase of a wave?
    a. The height of a wave in 2π radians.
    b. The length of a wave in 2π radians.
    c. The period of oscillation of a wave.
    d. An angle indicating the wave cycle's instantaneous location.

15. Which of the following statements is true about the acceleration of a simple pendulum?
    a. The acceleration is constant.
    b. The magnitude of the acceleration is at a maximum when the bob is at the bottom of the path.
    c. The magnitude of the acceleration is at a maximum when the bob is changing directions.
    d. None of the above.

16. Two waves, each of which has an amplitude of A, cross paths. At the point where they cross, the peak of one wave meets the trough of another wave. What is the resulting amplitude at the point where the waves cross?
    a. 0
    b. A
    c. 2A
    d. -A

17. Two tuning forks have a frequency of 500 Hz and 504 Hz and the same amplitude. How much time is there between beats?
    a. 4 seconds
    b. 15 seconds
    c. 0.25 seconds
    d. 2 seconds

18. Substance A has a density of 5.0 kg/m³ and substance B has a density of 4.0 kg/m³. What is the ratio of the volume A to volume B when the masses of the two substances are equal?
    a. 1.25
    b. 0.80
    c. 1.12
    d. 0.89

19. The center of a circular aquarium window with a radius 1 meter is 14 meters below the surface. What is the force of the water at this depth pushing on this window? The density of water is 1000 kg/m³.
    a. 1.37×10^5 newtons
    b. 1.08×10^5 newtons
    c. 4.3×10^5 newtons
    d. 0 newtons

20. The air passing over an airplane's wind is considered an irrotational fluid flow. Which of the following statements correctly describes the concept of irrotational fluid flow?
    a. The fluid flows in a straight line.
    b. All particles have the same velocity as they pass a particular point.
    c. A tiny paddle wheel placed in the fluid will rotate.
    d. The fluid does not have any rotating points, whirlpools or eddies.

21. Which statement best explains why water expands when it freezes?
    a. The coefficient of thermal expansion is negative.
    b. The average distance between the water molecules increases.
    c. The density of water is greater at higher temperatures.
    d. The internal energy of the water decreases.

22. Which of the following statements best describes the electric field shown below.

    a. The field is decreasing down.
    b. The field is decreasing to the right.
    c. The field is increasing to the right.
    d. The field is uniform.

23. An electric field is pointing from south to north. If a dipole is placed in the field, how will the dipole's orientation change?
    a. The positive charge will be on the northern side and the negative charge will be on the southern side.
    b. The positive charge will be on the southern side and the negative charge will be on the northern side.
    c. The positive charge will be on the eastern side and the negative charge will be on the western side.
    d. There will be no change in the orientation.

24. A magnetic field is directed into this page and an electron is moving from left to right as indicated in the diagram below.

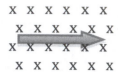

In which direction will the electron move when it enters the magnetic field?
a. It will curve upward.
b. It will curve downward.
c. It will curve in the direction of the magnetic field.
d. It will curve in the direction opposite the magnetic field.

25. In the 19th century, James Clerk Maxwell calculated the speed of light in a vacuum from the proportionality constants used in electrostatics and magnetism. Which of the following relationships correctly identifies how light moves in a vacuum?
a. High frequencies of light travel faster than low frequencies.
b. Low frequencies of light travel faster than high frequencies.
c. All frequencies of light travel at the same speed in a vacuum.
d. Light moves at infinite speed through a vacuum.

26. The diagram below shows two batteries connected in series to a resistor. What is the direction of current flow?

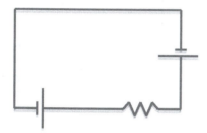

a. clockwise
b. counterclockwise
c. neither clockwise nor counterclockwise
d. Can't be determined from the information given.

27. A circuit consists of a battery and a resistor. An ammeter is used to measure the current in the circuit and is connected in series to the circuit. Which of the following is true?
a. The current flowing in the resistor increases.
b. The current flowing in the resistor decreases.
c. The voltage drop across the resistor increases.
d. The current flowing in the resistor remains the same.

28. A capacitor is connected in series to a battery and a resistor. The battery is disconnected after the capacitor is charged and replaced by a battery with a greater electromotive force, causing the capacitor to gain additional charge. After the capacitor has fully charged again, which of the following statements is true about the capacitance of the circuit?
   a. It has increased.
   b. It has decreased.
   c. It has remained the same.
   d. It has become zero.

29. A homemade generator rotates at a constant frequency and produces an alternating current with a maximum voltage of 40 volts. It is connected to a resistor of 20 ohms. What is the average current that flows through the resistor?
   a. 0 amperes.
   b. 1.4 amperes
   c. 2.0 amperes
   d. 2.8 amperes

30. A ray of light travelling in a vacuum (n = 1) is incident upon a glass plate (n = 1.3). It hits with an angle of incidence of 45°. If the angle of incidence increases to 50°, what is the new angle of refraction?
   a. It is 45°
   b. It is 50°
   c. It is below 45°
   d. It is above 50°

31. An object is placed a certain distance away from a convex spherical mirror. Which of the following statements is true?
   a. No image is formed.
   b. The image will be larger or smaller, depending on the object's distance from the mirror.
   c. The image will be smaller and right side up.
   d. The image will be smaller and either right side up or upside down, depending on the object's distance from the mirror.

32. An object with a net charge is brought into the vicinity of an object with a net charge of zero coulombs. Which statement describes the electrostatic force between the two objects?
   a. It is a repulsive force.
   b. It is an attractive force.
   c. There is no force.
   d. It is a perpendicular force.

33. Which of the following is the correct definition of a conductor?
    a. A metal wire in an electrical circuit.
    b. A material that contains moveable electric charges.
    c. A material that is not a semiconductor or insulator.
    d. Any device that allows electricity to flow.

34. A plastic comb is used to comb someone's dry hair and acquires a large positive charge. The comb is brought close to a small bit of uncharged paper lying on a table. Against the force of gravity, the bit of paper jumps up and sticks to the comb. What is likely to happen next?
    a. The paper will stick to the comb indefinitely.
    b. Air will eventually cause the comb to lose its charge and the paper will fall from the comb under the force of gravity.
    c. The paper will acquire a positive charge and be repelled by the comb.
    d. The paper will acquire a negative charge and be repelled by the comb.

35. When light from a single source strikes two slits, alternating bright and dark lines appear on a screen on the far side. What is the best explanation for this phenomenon?
    a. Doppler shift
    b. Diffraction and interference
    c. Chromatic aberration
    d. Total internal reflection

36. Which of the following phenomena implies that light consists of specific quanta?
    a. ultraviolet catastrophe
    b. threshold frequency
    c. emission of light
    d. stability of atoms

37. Which of the following statements about the image created by a magnifying glass is true?
    a. The image is always upside down.
    b. The image is always right side up.
    c. The image may be right side up or upside down, depending on the location of the object.
    d. The image may be right side up or upside down, depending on the thickness of the lens.

38. Suppose your actual weight is 150 pounds and you weigh yourself with an analog scale and get a reading of 152.1 pounds. You repeat the measurement twice more and get 152.1 pounds each time. Which of the following statements is true?
    a. There is no random error.
    b. There is no systematic error.
    c. The systematic error is 2.1 pounds.
    d. The random error is 2.1 pounds.

39. Which of the following statements is not a principle used in constructing ray diagrams to show the creation of images using a thin convex lens?

a. A ray parallel to the optical axis is refracted so that it goes through the focal point of the lens.

b. A ray that goes through the focal point of a lens and strikes the lens is refracted parallel to the optical axis.

c. A ray that goes through the center of a lens is not deflected.

d. A ray that strikes the surface of a lens follows Snell's law for refraction.

40. Which of the following devices changes chemical energy into electrical energy?

a. battery

b. closed electric circuit

c. generator

d. transformer

Quantitative Reasoning

1. What is the product of .34 x .06?
   a. 0.0204
   b. 0.204
   c. 2.04
   d. 20.4

2. If 8 people can eat 6 bags of chips, how many people will it take to eat 15 bags of chips?
   a. 16
   b. 18
   c. 20
   d. 22

3. Express 8% as a fraction.
   a. 4/100
   b. 4/25
   c. 2/25
   d. 2/50

4. Which algebraic expression best represents the following statement: the number of books Brian read over the summer (B) is 2 less than 3 times the number of books his brother Adam read over the summer (A)?
   a. B = 3A – 2
   b. B = 3A + 2
   c. A = 3B – 2
   d. A = 3B + 2

5. Stefan's scores on his English essays were 75, 65, 80, 95, and 65. What is the average of his test scores?
   a. 65
   b. 66
   c. 71
   d. 76

6. Multiply 3 1/4 x 8/18.
   a. 3 1/9
   b. 1 4/9
   c. 1/3
   d. 1/13

7. Ma'Tia drove 400 miles in 6 hours. She has an additional 180 miles to drive. If she drives at the same rate of speed, how long will it take her rounded to the nearest hour?

    a. 1 hour

    b. 2 hours

    c. 3 hours

    d. 4 hours

8. Mary's karate class has 7 students with white belts and 21 students with green belts. What is the ratio of students with white belts to all the students in the class?

    a. 7 to 21

    b. 4 to 1

    c. 1 to 3

    d. 1 to 4

9. What is the solution for the equation $x/3 + 4 = 7$

    a. 21

    b. 15

    c. 12

    d. 9

10. A small t-shirt store sells two different kinds of shirts: short sleeve cost $15.00 and long sleeve cost $18.00. If the store sold 21 shirts last night and made $351, how many of each kind of shirt did the store sell?

    a. 9 short sleeve and 12 long sleeve

    b. 8 short sleeve and 11 long sleeve

    c. 7 short sleeve and 10 long sleeve

    d. 6 short sleeve and 9 long sleeve

Lex's favorite cookie store sells the following cookies:

Sugar: $2.00

Macaroons: $1.50

Chocolate chip: $2.50

Peanut butter: $2.00

11. If Lex buys 3 cookies, what is the least amount he could have spent?

    a. $4.00

    b. $4.50

    c. $5.00

    d. $5.50

12. Lex's mom buys 3 of each kind of cookie for a picnic. If the store gives a 10% discount for purchase of a dozen cookies, how much did she spend?
    a. $21.60
    b. $22.60
    c. $23.00
    d. $24.00

13. How much do you save on a purchase of $47.00 if you shop in a store on a day in which the promotion is that the store will pay the sales tax (and sales tax is 8%)?
    a. $0.37
    b. $2.76
    c. $3.76
    d. $4.76

14. A pizza dough recipe calls for 2 cups of flour and 1 1/2 teaspoons of salt. How much salt would you need if you wanted to triple the recipe?
    a. 1 tablespoon
    b. 3 teaspoons
    c. 4 1/2 teaspoons
    d. 6 teaspoons

15. What does $4x - 1/2y$ equal if $x = 9$ and $y = 6$
    a. 36
    b. 33
    c. 30
    d. 26

16. What is the product of the numbers 0.007 and 7.5?
    a. 0.00525
    b. 0.0525
    c. 0.525
    d. 5.25

17. If Sherry won a sweepstakes that gave her $1000 a day for every non-weekend day, approximately how much money would she be given in one year?
    a. $365,000
    b. $260,000
    c. $52,000
    d. $24,000

18. The five events hosted last year by the event company, "We Plan It," drew crowds of 175, 320, 417, 533, and 210 people. What is their average attendance for those events?
    a. 231
    b. 271
    c. 331
    d. 371

19. If my local grocery store last year had a total income of $7,056,238 and expenses of $3,998,100, how much profit did it make (profit is income minus expenses)?
    a. $3,058,138
    b. $3,158,138
    c. $2,738,188
    d. $4,158,188

20. Which of the following is true?
    a. -(-(-4)) is greater than -3
    b. -(-(-7)) is greater than -17 plus 10
    c. -4 is greater than the absolute value of -4
    d. -10 is greater than -(-(-15))

21. What do you get if you subtract -4 – (-9)?
    a. 5
    b. -5
    c. -13
    d. 13

22. What is 60 divided by (-4)?
    a. -15
    b. 15
    c. -12
    d. 12

23. 184,770 is the product of 12,318 and what other number
    a. 13
    b. 14
    c. 15
    d. 16

24. What is 7 – 5 6/13?
    a. 2 3/13
    b. 2 1/13
    c. 1 9/13
    d. 1 7/13

25. Tyler is one year older than 3 times Clay's age. The sum of their ages is 21. How old is Tyler?
    a. 6
    b. 16
    c. 5
    d. 15

26. 24 is 60% of what number?
    a. 40
    b. 48
    c. 60
    d. 68

27. What is 0.09356 – 0.003784?
    a. 0.00089776
    b. 0.0089776
    c. 0.089776
    d. 0.89776

28. If the 8 people in the room wearing jeans constitute 40% of the people in the room, how many people are there total in the room?
    a. 60
    b. 40
    c. 20
    d. 10

29. If you travel at a rate of 65 mph, how many hours will it take you to travel 260 miles?
    a. 7
    b. 6
    c. 5
    d. 4

30. Jerome wants to enlarge his favorite painting by 20% (length and width). If it is currently 20 inches by 30 inches, what will the area of the enlarged painting be?
    a. 600 inches
    b. 864 inches
    c. 726 inches
    d. 926 inches

31. How many inches are in 4 1/3 yards?
    a. 96
    b. 106
    c. 126
    d. 156

32. What is the product of (-4)(-2)(-6)?
    a. -24
    b. 24
    c. -48
    d. 48

33. How many cubic inches are in a box 10" wide, 3" deep and 14" long?
    a. 420
    b. 4200
    c. 210
    d. 2100

34. What is the perimeter of a park that is 300 yards long and 640 yards wide?
    a. 1880
    b. 192,000
    c. 940
    d. 19,200

35. Solve the equation: $2^3 + (4 + 1)$.
    a. 9
    b. 13
    c. 15
    d. 21

36. What is the product of the numbers 3.75 and 0.004
    a. 0.015
    b. 0.15
    c. 1.5
    d. 15

37. If one yard equals three feet, how many feet are there in 7 2/3 yards?
    a. 2.5
    b. 21
    c. 23
    d. 25

38. Perform the following operation: 7 5/8 divided by 3 3/4.
    a. 2 1/30
    b. 2 7/30
    c. 3 1/30
    d. 3 7/30

39. If the average of 7 and x is equal to the average of 9, 4, and x, what is the value of x?
    a. 4
    b. 5
    c. 6
    d. 7
    e. 8

40. If four friends had an average score of 92 on a test, what was Annie's score if Bill got an 86, Clive got a 98 and Demetrius got a 90?
    a. 88
    b. 90
    c. 92
    d. 94
    e. 96

Answers and Explanations

Natural Science

Biology

1. D: An exothermic reaction releases energy, whereas an endothermic reaction requires energy. The breakdown of a chemical compound is an example of a decomposition reaction (AB → A + B.. A combination reaction (A + B →AB. is the reverse of a decomposition reaction, and a replacement (displacement) reaction is one where compound breaks apart and forms a new compound plus a free reactant (AB + C →AC + B or AB + CD → AD + CB.

2. B: Some RNA molecules in extant organisms have enzymatic activity; for example the formation of peptide bonds on ribosomes is catalyzed by an RNA molecule. This and other information has led scientists to believe that the most likely molecules to first demonstrate enzymatic activity were RNA molecules.

3. D: Enzyme inhibitors attach to an enzyme and block substrates from entering the active site, thereby preventing enzyme activity. As stated in the question, cyanide is a poison that irreversibly binds to an enzyme and blocks its active site, thus fitting the definition of an enzyme inhibitor.

4. E: Electrons trapped by the chlorophyll P680 molecule in photosystem II are energized by light. They are then transferred to electron acceptors in an electron transport chain.

5. C: The synaptonemal complex is the point of contact between homologous chromatids. It is formed when nonsister chromatids exchange genetic material through crossing over. Once prophase of meiosis I has completed, crossovers have resolved and the synaptonemal complex no longer exists. Rather, sister chromatids are held together at their centromeres prior to separation in anaphase II.

6. A: Monocots differ from dicots in that they have one cotyledon, or embryonic leaf in their embryos. They also have parallel veination, fibrous roots, petals in multiples of three, and a random arrangement of vascular bundles in their stems.

7. B: In ferns, the mature diploid plant is called a sporophyte. Sporophytes undergo meiosis to produce spores, which develop into gametophytes, which produce gametes.

8. B: Anthers produce microspores (the male gametophytes of flowering plants), which undergo meiosis to produce pollen grains.

- 49 -

9. C: In flowering plants, the anthers house the male gametophytes (which produce sperm) and the pistils house the female gametophytes (which produce eggs). Eggs and sperm are haploid. All other tissues are solely diploid.

10. C: In a positive feedback loop, an action intensifies a chain of events that, in turn, intensify the conditions that caused the action beyond normal limits. Nursing stimulates lactation, which promotes nursing. Contractions during childbirth, psychological hysteria, and sexual orgasm are all examples of positive feedback.

11. B: The gastrula is formed from the blastocyst, which contains a bilayered embryonic disc. One layer of this disc's inner cell mass further subdivides into the epiblast and the hypoblast, resulting in the three primary germ layers (endoderm, mesoderm, ectoderm).

12. A: Vultures eat carrion, or dead animals, so they are considered scavengers. Detritivores are heterotrophs that eat decomposing organic matter such as leaf litter. They are usually small.

13. B: The growth rate is equal to the difference between births and deaths divided by population size.

14. D: Within a habitat, there is a maximum number of individuals that can continue to thrive, known as the habitat's carrying capacity. When the population size approaches this number, population growth will stop.

15. B: Phyletic gradualism is the view that evolution occurs at a more or less constant rate. Contrary to this view, punctuated equilibrium holds that evolutionary history consists of long periods of stasis punctuated by geologically short periods of evolution. This theory predicts that there will be few fossils revealing intermediate stages of evolution, whereas phyletic gradualism views the lack of intermediate-stage fossils as a deficit in the fossil record that will resolve when enough specimens are collected.

16. B: The bottleneck effect occurs when populations undergo a dramatic decrease in size. It could be due to natural or artificial causes.

17. C: Plants have cellulose as the major structural component of their cell walls. However, plants store energy as starch, not cellulose. Starch is a polymer of α-glucose molecules, whereas cellulose is a polymer of β-glucose molecules. The different chemical bonds between glucose molecules in starch and cellulose make the difference in whether or not the polymer is digestible in plants and animals.

18. E: Triglycerides are hydrophobic. They consist of three fatty acids joined to a glycerol molecule, and because of their long hydrocarbon chains, they are not soluble in water.

19. B: This is an example of negative feedback, a process whereby an increase in an outcome causes a decrease or slowing in the pathways that led to the outcome.

20. A: A cofactor binds to the active site along with the substrate in order to catalyze an enzymatic reaction. Like the enzyme, it is not consumed by the reaction. Allosteric effectors bind to a second binding site on the enzyme, not the active site.

21. B: Water and carbon dioxide are the two essential consumable molecules in photosynthesis. First, water is split into oxygen, protons, and electrons, and then carbon dioxide is used in the Calvin cycle to create glucose. The electrons from splitting water are used in photosystem II, the protons are used to create NADPH, and oxygen is a waste product of the splitting of water.

22. B: Auxin is found in higher concentrations on the shaded side than the sunny side of a stem. More elongation on the shaded side causes the stem to bend toward the light.

23. D: Insects and most mollusks have open circulatory systems. Vertebrates, the phylum Annelida (earthworms), and some mollusks (squid and octopuses) have closed circulatory systems.

24. D: In negative feedback, when a pathway's output (increased blood glucose) exceeds normal limits, a mechanism is activated that reduces inputs to the pathway (reduction of blood glucose). Conditions are monitored by a control center, and when homeostasis returns, the corrective action is discontinued.

25. C: Gametes are haploid and have only one allele. Half the gametes from this individual will have the T allele and half will have the t allele.

26. B: Sex-linked, or X-linked, traits can only be transmitted to males through the mother.

27. B: Plants and animals cannot use inorganic nitrogen. It must be fixed, or reduced to ammonium, in order to enter a living ecosystem.

28. C: The carrying capacity is the maximum number of individuals a habitat can sustain, so when the population size reaches this number, growth will stop.

29. B: Selection that favors one extreme trait over all others is called directional selection. If directional selection continues for many generations, the population will end up with only one allele for that trait.

30. C: According to Hardy-Weinberg equilibrium, $p + q = 1$ and $p^2 + 2pq + q^2 = 1$. In this scenario, $q^2 = 0.25$, so $q = 0.5$. p must also be 0.5. $2pq$ is equal to $2(.5)(.5)$ or 0.5.

31. B: Simple molecules were able to form in the earth's early atmosphere because oxygen was absent. Oxygen is very reactive and it would have supplanted other molecules in chemical reactions if it were present.

32. D: Enzymes are substrate-specific. Most enzymes catalyze only one biochemical reaction. Their active sites are specific for a certain type of substrate and do not bind to other substrates and catalyze other reactions.

33. D: The enzyme helicase unwinds DNA. It depends on several other proteins to make the unwinding run smoothly, however. Single-strand binding protein holds the single stranded DNA in place, and topoisomerase helps relieve tension at the replication fork.

34. A: DNA synthesis on the lagging strand forms short segments called Okazaki fragments. Because DNA polymerase can only add nucleotides in the $5' \rightarrow 3'$ direction, lagging strand synthesis is discontinuous. The final product is formed when DNA ligase joins Okazaki fragments together.

35. A: Transcription is the process of creating an RNA strand from a DNA template. All forms of RNA, for example mRNA, tRNA, and rRNA, are products of transcription.

36. D: Mammals often warm themselves by altering their metabolism. Shivering warms animals due to the heat generated by contractions in trunk muscles.

37. E: The testes contain hundreds of seminiferous tubules for the production of sperm, or spermatogenesis. This requires 64-72 days. Leydig cells surround the seminiferous tubules and produce male sex hormones called androgens, the most important of which is testosterone. Semen is made in the seminal vesicles, prostate gland, and other glands. Sperm are transferred to the penis via the epididymis, where they become motile, and thence through the vas deferens.

38. C: Half of the boys will receive the color-blind allele from the mother, and the other half will receive the normal one. All the girls will receive the color-blind allele from the father; half of them will also get one from the mother, while the other half will get the normal one. Therefore, half the children will be colorblind.

39. B: When more than one gene contributes to a trait, inheritance of that trait is said to be polygenic. This type of inheritance does not follow the rules of Mendelian genetics.

40. D: The parents in D could only have offspring with AB or B blood types, not the A blood type.

General Chemistry

1. D: Generally, the larger and heavier the molecule, the higher the melting point. Decreasing polarity will lower intermolecular attractions and lower the melting point. Long, linear molecules have a larger surface area, and therefore more opportunity to interact with other molecules, which increases the melting point.

2. D: Since there are twice as many molecules of hydrogen present vs. oxygen, the partial pressure of hydrogen will be greater. The mass of hydrogen will not be greater than the mass of oxygen present even though there are more moles of hydrogen, due to oxygen having a higher molecular weight. Each gas will occupy the same volume. Hydrogen and oxygen gas can coexist in the container without reacting to produce water. There is no indication given that a chemical reaction has occurred.

3. B: Plugging the data into the ideal gas law using the correct units gives the correct answer in atmospheres, which in this case is 2.4 atm. The equation is $P = nRT/V$. So we have $P = 1$ mol $(0.08206$ L atm/mol K$)(298$ K$)/10$ L. The R value is 0.08206 L atm/mol K when using L as the volume unit, and delivers the pressure in atm.

4. D: Both liquids and gases are fluids and therefore flow, but only gases are compressible. The molecules that make up a gas are very far apart, allowing the gas to be compressed into a smaller volume.

5. C: As the temperature drops to -5 °C, the water vapor condenses to a liquid, and then to a solid. The vapor pressure of a solid is much less than that of the corresponding gas. The argon is still a gas at -5 °C, so almost all the pressure in the cylinder is due to argon.

6. D: $AgNO_3$, $NaNO_3$ and $NaCl$ are all highly water soluble and would not precipitate under these conditions. All nitrate compounds and compounds containing Group I metals are soluble in water. $AgCl$ is essentially insoluble in water, and this is the precipitate observed.

7. B: Pure water boils at 100 °C. Water that has salts dissolved in it will boil at a slightly higher temperature, and will conduct electricity much better than pure water.

8. A: The weight % of the acetic acid is the mass of acetic acid divided by the mass of the acetic acid plus the water. So 50g/(50g +200g) = 0.2, or 20%. The mole fraction is the moles of acetic acid divided by the total number of moles of the solution. So 50 g of acetic acid (MW = 60) is 50g/ 60 g/mol = 0.83 moles. 200 g of water = 11.11 moles. Therefore, 0.83 mol/(0.83 mol + 11.11 mol) = 0.069.

9. A: Since we have 1 liter of the solution, then 0.02 M represents 0.02 moles of methanol. The mass of methanol can then be found by 0.02mol x MW of CH_3OH (32) = 0.64 g. Molality is the moles of solute (methanol) divided by the number of kilograms of solvent, in this case, it is essentially 1 kg. This is assumed since the solvent is water and the density of water is 1 g/mL. So 0.02 mol/ 1 kg = 0.02 m.

10. C: Since each half life is 2 years, eight years would be 4 half lives. So the mass of material is halved 4 times. Therefore if we start with 1 kg, at two years we would have 0.5 kg, at four years we would have 0.25 kg, after 6 years we would have 0.12 kg, and after 8 years we would have 0.06 kg.

11. A: Nuclear reactions convert mass into energy ($E = mc^2$). The mass of products is always less than that of the starting materials since some mass is now energy.

12. C: Hund's rule states that electrons must populate empty orbitals of similar energy before pairing up. The Aufbau principle states that electrons must fill lower energy orbitals before filling higher energy orbitals. The Pauli exclusion principle states that no two electrons in the same atom can have the same four quantum numbers, and therefore, two electrons in the same orbital will have opposite spins.

13. A: NaCl is an ionic salt, and therefore the most polar. F_2 is nonpolar since the two atoms share the electrons in an equal and symmetrical manner. CH_3OH is an alcohol with a very polar O-H bond. CH_3CH_2Cl is also a polar molecule due to the unequal sharing of electrons between in the C-Cl bond.

14. D: The correct structure of ammonium sulfate is $(NH_4)_2SO_4$. Its molecular weight is 132. The masses of the elements in the compound are: nitrogen 28 (2 x 14), hydrogen 8 (1x8), sulfur 32 (32x1) and oxygen 64 (16x4). To find the percentage composition of each element, divide the element mass by the molecular weight of the compound and multiply by 100. So nitrogen is (28/132)x100 = 21%, hydrogen is (8/132)x100 = 6%, sulfur is (32/132)x100 = 24% and oxygen is (64/132)x100 = 48%.

15. D: 1 kg of heptane (MW 100) is equal to 10 moles of heptane. Since 8 moles of water is produced for every mole of heptane reacted, 80 moles of water must be produced. 80 moles of water (MW 18) equals 1440 g, or 1.4 kg.

16. B: Since the conversion of B to C is the slow step, this is the only one that determines the reaction rate law. Therefore, the rate law will be based on B, since it is the only reactant in producing C.

17. A: Lewis acids are compounds capable of accepting a lone pair of electrons. $AlCl_3$ is a very strong Lewis acid and can readily accept a pair of electrons due to Al only having 6 electrons instead of 8 in its outer shell. $FeCl_3$ is also a strong Lewis acid, though milder than $AlCl_3$. Sulfuric acid is a Bronsted-Lowry acid since it produces protons. PCl_3 is a Lewis base since the P can donate its lone pair of electrons to another species.

18. B: The K_a of acetic acid is determined from the pK_a, $K_a = 10^{-pka} = 1.75 \times 10^{-5}$. This is the equilibrium constant for the acetic acid dissociation, or $K_a = [H^+][CH_3COO^-]/[CH_3COOH]$. Using this equilibrium equation to solve for the $[H^+]$, the pH of the buffer can then be found. Solving for the $[H^+]$ concentration, we get $[H^+] = K_a \times [CH_3COOH]/CH_3COO^-]$, or $[H^+] = 1.75 \times 10^{-5} \times [0.1]/[0.2] = 8.75 \times 10^{-6}$. pH = $-\log[H^+]$ = 5.05.

19. C: Cooling means heat is leaving the system, so it must be negative. We have 5.9 mol of ammonia cooling 75 °C, or 75 K. So 5.9 mol x -75 K x 35.1 J/(mol)(K) = -15.5 kJ.

20. C: The first is an alkyne, which contains a triple bond between carbon atoms. The second is a ketone and contains a carbon-oxygen double bond. The third is an alkene, which has a double bond between two carbon atoms. The fourth is an imide, which contains a double bond between two nitrogen atoms.

21. D: Combustion of coal releases significant amounts of Hg into the atmosphere. When the Hg settles into the water, it becomes methylated and concentrates in fish, making them toxic to eat.

22. A: The higher the temperature of the liquid, the greater the solubility of the solid, while the higher the temperature, the lower the solubility of the gas.

23. C: Catalysts lower the energy barrier between products and reactants and thus increase the reaction rate.

24. B: NH_3 is ammonia, which is a base. H_2O is amphoteric, meaning that it can act as either a weak acid or a weak base. HF is actually a weak acid, despite fluorine being the most electronegative atom. The small size of the F results in a stronger bond between the H and F, which reduces acidity since this bond will be harder to break. H_3PO_4, phosphoric acid, is high in acidity and HCl is a very strong acid, meaning it completely dissociates.

25. D: To make a buffer, a weak acid and its conjugate base or a weak base and its conjugate acid are commonly used. Buffers work by using the common-ion effect and result in little change in the pH when an acid or a base is added. HCl/NaOH is a strong acid/strong base combination and will not result in a buffer solution. Although the HNO_3/$NaNO_3$ and H_2SO_4/$NaHSO_4$ mixtures are conjugate acid/base pairs, both HNO_3 and H_2SO_4 are strong acids, not weak acids. Neither of these solutions would result in a buffer. Only the NaH_2PO_4/Na_2HPO_4 mixture would result in a buffer as it is a combination of a weak acid and its conjugate base.

26. A: The heat of combustion is determined by subtracting the heats of formation of the reactants from that of the products. So 3(-393.5) + 4(-285.8) – (-103.8) = -2220.

27. C: Because all unique materials have differing heat capacities, no two can heat up the same way. All will require different amounts of heat to warm to the same temperature.

28. D: Lead (Pb) goes from a zero oxidation state to a 2+ oxidation state, and is therefore oxidized. Oxidation is the loss of electrons. Hydrogen goes from a 1+ oxidation state to a 0 oxidation state, and is therefore reduced. Reduction is the gaining of electrons.

29. C: Reducing agents give up electrons to another chemical species, which cause that species to gain an electron and become reduced. Oxidizing agents cause another species to be oxidized, or to lose an electron, and are themselves reduced as they gain that electron. Bromine is very electronegative, and is almost always an oxidizing agent. N_2 is nearly inert, or unreactive. Neon is an inert noble gas and would not be a reducing agent. Sodium (Na) is

very reactive and eager to give up an electron, and is therefore a good reducing agent in a wide variety of reactions.

30. C: Reduction takes place at the cathode and oxidation takes place at the anode. Mg^{2+} of the salt will be reduced to $Mg(0)$ at the cathode, and Cl^- will be oxidized to Cl_2 at the anode.

Organic Chemistry

1. B: The general molecular formula for alkanes is C_nH_{2n+2}. Each carbon atom requires two hydrogen atoms and there must be two additional hydrogen atoms to complete the required total number of bonds to the terminal sp^3 carbon atoms.

2. D: Pure compounds are characterized by having sharp melting points. Eutectic mixtures are also characterized by a distinct melting point associated with a specific combination of two or more different compounds. Thus a sharp melting point is not sufficient by itself to identify an unknown substance as a pure compound. Only b) and c) can be unequivocally true statements

3. C: Only the s and p orbitals of the same principal quantum level are sufficiently close in energy to combine and form the hybrid sp^3 orbitals. The sp orbital is a hybrid of the s orbital and one of the p orbitals of the same principal quantum level. Therefore, the $3s$ and one $3p$ orbital would form the $3sp$ hybrid orbital, not the sp^3 orbital.

4. C: Propanol is the alcohol $H_3CCH_2CH_2OH$, molecular weight = 60 g/mole. Propanal is the aldehyde, H_3CCH_2CHO, molecular weight = 58 g/mole.
Propanone is the ketone H_3CCOCH_3, commonly known as acetone, molecular weight = 58 g/mole. All three are readily reactive molecules, and all three structures are based on a backbone of three carbon atoms. Only answer c) is true.

5. A: Acids and alcohols react to form esters by the elimination of the components of the water molecule from the two. In this reaction, the –OH from the acid and the –H from the alcohol "condense" to form a molecule of HO-H, or H_2O.

6. B: The Z- designation stands for "zusammen" (German, "the same") and indicates that the two high priority substituents are located on the same side of the molecular structure relative to each other. The E- designation stands for "entgegen" (German, "opposite") and indicates that the high priority substituents are located on opposite sides of the molecular structure relative to each other.
The R- and d,l designations indicate the absolute configuration and the direction of optical rotation about an asymmetric sp^3 carbon atom.

7. A: An sp^2 carbon atom has three substituents in a trigonal planar geometry. The carbonium ion is a prime example. As a fourth substituent bond forms, the atom changes its hybridization from trigonal sp^2 to tetrahedral sp^3. The fourth bond can form on either face of the sp^2 arrangement to generate either a left-handed or right-handed tetrahedral

arrangement of four different substituents. The three substituents on the sp^2 center must be different from each other and from the fourth substituent for this to be true. An sp^2 carbon atom that meets these requirements has the potential to form a chiral sp^3 center and is therefore referred to as prochiral.

"Delocalized" refers to the ability of electrons to move through adjacent p orbitals that are subject to sideways overlap.

"Stabilized" refers to the electronic influence exerted by substituents that imparts greater stability to a particular structure.

"Resonance structures" are equivalent arrangements of the bonds in a molecule.

8. A: The *d,l*- designation is not generally used since its meaning was deemed to be ambiguous. The term "racemate" is used when the mixture contains equal quantities of molecules that are individually mirror images of each other, or enantiomers. The term "lone pair" refers to a pair of valence electrons on an atom that are not involved in bonding. A *meso*- structure is a molecule in which two chiral centers exist across a plane of symmetry in enantiomeric configurations.

9. D: The carbonyl group is a characteristic feature common to all aldehydes, ketones and carboxylic acid derivatives. The carbonyl group is a carbon double bonded to an oxygen (C=O). Amides also contain a carbonyl group bonded to a N atom.

10. D: Proton signals in NMR exhibit "spin splitting" according to the number of different protons on adjacent carbon atoms. Protons experiencing identical magnetic environments produce identical signals, so the three protons of a single methyl group produce just one peak at about $\delta1.0$. In an ethyl group, $-CH_2CH_3$, the three methyl protons are affected by the two $-CH_2-$ protons and their signal is split into three slightly different peaks called a "triplet". The $-CH_2-$ proton signal is split by the three $-CH_3$ protons into four slightly different peaks called a quartet. Integration of the quartet and the triplet sets of peaks is in the ratio of 2:3 respectively, according to the number of each different type of proton. There is certainly one ethyl group present indicated by this pattern, but it does not preclude the possibility that there may be two or more identical ethyl groups in the molecule. They would still have a 2:3 integration ratio, so in this case the correct answer is d).

11. C: The permanganate ion coordinates to a C=C bond and subsequently transfers two O atoms to the alkene carbon atoms. The process requires base catalysis in methanol solution and produces a compound in which the two C=C carbon atoms each acquire an –OH group. Compounds with an –OH group on each of two adjacent carbon atoms are called "vicinal" diols.

The reaction does not occur in hot acid solution, or with potassium dichromate.

12. C: Activated charcoal powder acts as an adsorbent. The molecules of colored impurities tend to be polar compounds that adhere to the surfaces of the charcoal powder. Subsequently, filtration to remove the charcoal powder also removes the colored impurities.

Filtration alone can only remove impurities that are present as solids, colored or otherwise. A cosolvent is used in recrystallization either to form a suitable solvent system or to initiate the formation of crystals.

Chromatography is a procedure for separating compounds in a mixture and is not part of the recrystallization process.

13. A: Cellulose is a biopolymer, which is a large molecule produced by the sequential linking of hundreds and thousands of individual glucose molecules. Glucose is a "simple sugar", a single carbohydrate molecule, so its polymeric form, cellulose, is also a carbohydrate. The names of all carbohydrate molecules end in –ose. Starch is also a carbohydrate. It is similar to cellulose but composed of shorter polymeric chains of sequential glucose molecules.

Levulose, also known as fructose, and mannose are also carbohydrates. Mannose is an epimer of glucose. Epimers are diastereomers that have multiple stereocenters, but they differ in configuration at only one.

Caffeine is an alkaloid, not a carbohydrate.

Gallic acid is a carboxylic acid, not a carbohydrate.

Pyridine, C_5H_5N, is a six-membered ring nitrogen heterocycle analogous to benzene, C_6H_6, and is not a carbohydrate.

14. C: A carbonyl compound with α protons can rearrange to an equivalent form that is only slightly less stable than the carbonyl structure. This second form is called an enol, because it has an –OH group attached to a C=C bond. The two forms are called "tautomers" and the process of interconversion between the two forms is keto – enol tautomerism.

Racemization is the formation of an equal mixture of two enantiomers.

Inversion is the reversal of the relative orientation of three substituents about an sp^3 carbon atom in an S_N2 substitution reaction mechanism.

Conformational isomerism is the ability of a molecule to exist in different shapes, for example, the *chair* and *boat* conformations of cyclohexane.

15. B: Friedel-Crafts reactions typically use a strong Lewis acid such as $AlCl_3$ or $FeCl_3$ as a catalyst. Hydrogen chloride is not effective as a catalyst for Friedel-Crafts reactions. Friedel-Crafts reactions are applicable to most aryl and aromatic compounds.

16. A: This is a Friedel-Crafts alkylation reaction, in which the benzyl group, $C_6H_5CH_2-$, replaces an H atom on the benzene ring to form diphenylmethane, $C_6H_5CH_2C_6H_5$

17. A: Amides are formed by the replacement of an amine H atom by the acyl group of an acyl halide. Only amines with H atoms bonded to the amine N atom can undergo this reaction to produce an amide, so only primary and secondary amines can react in this way to produce amides.

Tertiary amines can accept the acyl halide to form an acyl trialkylammonium salt, but not an amide.

18. C: Phosphorus is in the same group as nitrogen and forms analogous compounds. It has oxidation states of +3 in compounds such as phosphines and +5 in compounds such as phosphine oxides and phosphates.

19. C: This is a nucleophilic substitution reaction. The base extracts an α proton from 4-t-butylcyclohexanone to generate an enolate anion. This then acts as a nucleophile to replace the bromine atom of 1-bromobutane. The reaction "alkylates" the 4-t-butylcyclohexanone molecule. The second equivalent of base allows the reaction to occur a second time, alkylating the cyclohexanone again on the opposite side of the carbonyl group.

20. B: Proteins are biopolymers of amino acids connected head-to-tail through peptide bonds (amide structures). The sequential order of the amino acids in the protein molecule is designated as the primary structure of the protein.
The folding of the molecule at specific amino acid locations is designated as the secondary structure of the protein molecule, and is due to the relative positions of the amino acids according to bond angles. This also determines the fundamental geometry of cavities and other features in the overall structure. Hydrogen bonding also plays an important role in the folding of the peptide chain in the secondary structure.

21. C: The initial step of a Birch reduction is the preparation of the Birch reducing agent by dissolving sodium metal in liquid ammonia. The intense blue color of the resulting solution is attributed to solvated electrons. Birch reduction is a very strong reduction method because the electrons act directly on the target molecule. The method readily reduces the benzene ring to a 1,4-cyclohexadiene system.
Birch reduction has nothing whatsoever to do with charcoal powder from birch wood. The active principle in Birch reduction is electrons dissolved in liquid ammonia from sodium metal. It is not sodium amide, $NaNH_2$, which is a very strong base.
Sodium metal in refluxing THF is a method of ensuring that the sodium contains no traces of dissolved water. That method is more effective when benzophenone, $C_6H_5COC_6H_5$, is added to the mixture, and a dark blue color is generated in the refluxing THF when benzophenone is present.

22. b. In an S_N2 reaction, a nucleophile approaches an sp^3 carbon center from the side opposite the substituent that it will replace. As it approaches, the bond to that "leaving group" weakens and a bond to the approaching nucleophile begins to form. As this change progresses, the hybridization of the atomic orbitals on the reactive center changes from sp^3 to $sp^2 + p$, and the other three substituents move into a trigonal planar array about the carbon atom in the transition state. As the bond continues to form to the nucleophile, the bond to the leaving group disappears and the hybridization of the central carbon atom becomes sp^3 again. The three substituents that were initially oriented toward the incoming nucleophile end up oriented away from it in the product structure. This is inversion of the stereochemistry.
The formation of a carbonium ion is characteristic of S_N1 and E1 reaction mechanisms. Alcohols can be produced by an S_N2 reaction, but so can many other types of compounds.

Carbon-carbon double bonds are formed in elimination reactions, not substitution reactions.

23. b. R-OH + TsOCl → R-OTs + HCl
           R-NH2 + TsOCl → R-NHTs + HCl
Tosylates are produced by the reaction of alcohols with p-toluenesulfonyl chloride, or tosyl chloride. The reaction of amines with tosyl chloride produces tosylamides. The reaction of a compound containing both an –OH group and an –NH$_2$ group with only one equivalent of tosyl chloride would produce a tosylamino alcohol. But this would only be true if the tosyl chloride was to react at the amine function instead of the alcohol function, and it would also be correctly termed a tosylamido alcohol and not a tosylamino alcohol.
Tosyl chloride is the reactant, not the product.

24. C: In a condensation reaction, two molecules are bonded to each other as the components of a water molecule are "condensed" from them. An –OH group is eliminated from one molecule and an H from the other, to produce H$_2$O as one of the products. When this occurs with carboxylic acids the acid anhydride is formed. "Anhydride" means "without water".
Acetic anhydride is specifically the anhydride of acetic acid.
A mixed anhydride is an anhydride formed from molecules of two different carboxylic acids, but these rarely form.
Maleic anhydride is specifically the anhydride of maleic acid.

25. B: Separation of compounds in distillation occurs because of their differential rates of evaporation and condensation equilibria. The more often the vapors in the apparatus can condense and evaporate, the more distinct the separation of the components will be.
The more quickly a distillation process is carried out, the less distinct the separation of the components will be, making the process less efficient.
A very cold condenser temperature has the effect of forcing the vapor through the system before it can condense and evaporate again, decreasing both the separation of the components and the efficiency of the process.
Reduced pressure decreases the temperatures at which the components will distill, without affecting the separation behavior.

26. C: "Aldo" indicates that the acyclic form is an aldehydes. "Hex" indicates a six-membered foundation structure, and "-ose" denotes that the compound is a carbohydrate or sugar.
The term "pentohexose" is a made-up term and has no meaning.
Lactose is a specific compound found in milk, also known as "milk sugar". Some people are not able to digest this sugar and are called "lactose intolerant".
Ketofuranose is a class of sugar molecules whose cyclic structure is based on the five-membered oxygen heterocyclic "furan" structure and whose acyclic or linear structure is a polyhydroxy ketone.

27. B: Furan is a five-membered oxygen heterocyclic compound. Sugar molecules that have this same basic skeletal structure are called furanose sugars.

Pyran is a six-membered ring analog of furan. Pyranose sugars have a cyclic structure based on the pyran ring.

A pentose is any five-carbon carbohydrate molecule.

Cyclohexose is a made-up term and has no meaning.

28. A: Disaccharides are carbohydrate molecules formed by the linking of two simple sugar molecules like glucose and fructose. The term "oligosaccharide" denotes short carbohydrate molecules typically composed of four or more simple sugar molecules.

The sucrose molecule has seven –OH groups, and dissolves quite readily in many organic solvents.

29. B: "Keto" denotes that the acyclic form is a ketone.

"Hex" denotes a six-carbon structure and "-ose" denotes that the compound is a carbohydrate.

Such compounds are well known. They do not contain both a C=C bond and a C=O group and are therefore not enones. Aldopentoses are five-carbon sugar molecules whose acyclic form is an aldehyde.

30.D: "Hetero" denotes that different atoms are present in the basic skeletal structure of the molecule.

"Cycle" denotes that the compound has a ring structure rather than a linear structure.

A "carbocycle" is a cyclic compound whose basic ring structure consists only of carbon atoms.

"Paracycles" is a made-up term and has no meaning.

"Macrocycles" are compounds whose basic structure is a large ring or cyclic structure.

Reading Comprehension

1. D
2. B
3. A
4. B
5. B
6. C
7. C
8. C
9. A
10. A
11. A
12. D
13. B

14. D
15. B
16. B
17. B
18. A
19. E
20. B
21. B
22. D
23. A
24. D
25. A
26. B
27. C
28. A
29. C
30. B
31. A
32. D
33. A
34. B
35. C
36. D
37. B
38. D
39. C
40. A

Physics

1. D: When adding, the answer will have as many significant figures after the decimal point as the measurement with the fewest decimal places. The total mass (ignoring significant figure) is obtained by adding up all four measurements. This yields B, not A. But since the first and second masses are precise to only a hundredth of a gram, your answer can't be more precise than this. The number 35.5918, when rounded to two significant figures after the decimal point (to match your measurement of 23.04) is 35.59.

2. C: To add and subtract vectors algebraically, you add and subtract their components. To add vectors graphically, you shift the location of the vectors so that they are connected tail-to-tail. The resultant is a vector that starts at the tail of the first vector and ends at the tip of the second. To subtract vectors, however, you connect the vectors tail-to-tail, not tip to tail, starting with the vector that is not subtracted, and ending with the one that is. Think of this just like vector addition, except the vector that is subtracted (the one with the negative sign in front of it) switches directions.

3. C: This is a problem of free-fall in two-dimensions. A thrown ball without air resistance will only be subjected to one force, gravity. This causes a downward acceleration of exactly 9.8 m/s^2 on all objects, regardless of their size, speed or position. Note: since the ball was thrown directly upwards, the HORIZONTAL acceleration is 0 m/s^2 and the horizontal speed at all times is 0 m/s. B is wrong because the force of gravity is always pointed downward and never changes direction.

4. B: The newton is defined in terms of the fundamental units meters, kilograms, and seconds (N = kg × m/s^2), so it is not a fundamental unit. II is a verbal statement of $F = ma$, Newton's second law, which is true. If $F = 0$ N, then the acceleration is 0 m/s^2. If the acceleration is 0 m/s^2, then the speed is 0 m/s or a nonzero constant. This is a nonverbal statement of Newton's first law, meaning Newton's first law can be derived from his second law. Newton's second law cannot be derived from the universal law of gravity.

5. C: The centripetal force pushes you in toward the center of the ring, not towards the wall. The centripetal force also causes the ring to push against you, which is why it might feel like you're being push outwards. This force also causes friction between your back and the wall, and that's why you don't fall when the floor is removed, assuming the frictional force is large enough to overcome gravity. As the speed of rotation increases, the force exerted by the wall on your body increases, so the frictional force between you and the wall increases. Answer B is correct—centripetal force does cause you to change direction—but it does not explain why you don't fall. Also note that "centrifugal force" is an illusion; because you feel the wall pushing against your back, you feel like you're being pushed outwards. In fact, you're being pulled inwards, but the wall is also being pulled inwards and is pushing against you. Finally, you are not weightless on a ride like this.

6. C: The question asks how much friction is needed to START the block moving, which means you need to calculate the force of static friction. If the question had asked about the force needed to KEEP the object moving at a constant speed, you would calculate the force of kinetic friction. Here, the force of static friction is equal to $\mu_{static} \times N$, where N is the Normal force. The normal force (N) on the plastic block is the weight of the block (mg) = 10 kg x 9.8 m/s^2 = 98 newtons. The force of static friction = 0.6 x 98N = 59 N. Answer B is the force of kinetic friction, once the block starts moving. (Note: molecular bonding and abrasion cause friction. When the surfaces are in motion the bonding is less strong, so the coefficient of kinetic friction is less than the coefficient of static friction. Therefore, more force is required to start the box moving than to keep it moving.)

7. B: The weight of the masses is determined from $W = mg$. In this case, there is a force to the left/down of 20 kg x 9.8 m/s^2 = 196 N, and a force to the right/down of 30 kg x 9.8 m/s^2 = 294 N. The net force is 98 N to the right/down. This force is moving both masses, however, which have a total mass of 50 kg. Using F = ma and solving for acceleration gives a = 98 N / 50 kg = 2 m/s^2.

8. B: The torque acting on an object is the force acting on the object (in this case, its weight = mg) times its distance from the pivot point. Here, the masses and the bar are balanced, so the net torque is 0 N × m. This means the clockwise torque is equal and opposite to the

counter clockwise torque ($m_1gd_1 = m_2gd_2$). Dividing the distance in half would only add a factor of ½ to both sides of this equation. Since this affects both sides equally, the net torque is still zero when both distances are halved. C would be the correct answer if the mass of the bar was not zero.

9. D: Impulse is the change in an object's momentum (mv), which is in units of kg x m/s. An object's impulse can change, depending on the forces acting upon it. For a ball rolling down a hill, gravity provides a constant force, which causes the ball to accelerate. This creates an impulse that increases as the ball gets faster and faster. This impulse does not exist for a short time, but will continue as long as the ball is accelerating.

10. B: Using conservation of momentum, the original eastward momentum = 75 x 5 = 375 kg m/s and the northward momentum is 100 x 4 = 400 kg m/s. Afterwards, the two skaters have a combined mass of 175 kg. Using the Pythagorean theorem (for a right triangle w/ hypotenuse A, $A^2 = B^2 + C^2$), their total momentum will be $\sqrt{(375^2 + 400^2)}$ = 548 KG M/S. Setting this equal to mv, 548 = (175) v, gives v = 3.1 m/s.

11. B: The work-energy theorem can be written $W = \Delta KE$. It is derived from Newton's second law ($F = ma$) by multiplying both sides by the distance the object moves. This work is the work done by a force on an object, and not the work done by an object. Work is only done by an object if that object exerts a force on another object, causing a change in its kinetic energy or position. The work done on an object MAY equal its potential energy, but only if that potential energy is converted into kinetic energy. In real-life cases, some energy is converted to heat, for example, so the change in potential energy does not equal the change in kinetic energy.

12. C: The initial gravitational potential energy of the ball is mgh, where h is the height above the ground. At the top of the loop, some of this energy will be converted into kinetic energy ($\frac{1}{2}mv_{top}^2$). Since its height is 2R at the top of the loop, it will have a potential energy here of $mg(2R)$. Using the conservation of energy: $mgh = \frac{1}{2}m\, v_{top}^2 + mg(2R)$. Additionally, in order to maintain a circular path, the centripetal force must equal the gravitational force at the top of the loop: $\frac{(m\, v_{top}^2)}{R} = mg$, which can be rewritten as $v_{top}^2 = gR$. Putting this into the energy equation, you find $mgh = \frac{1}{2}\, m(gR) + mg(2R)$. Dividing m and g from both sides of this equation shows that $h = \frac{1}{2}R + 2R = \frac{5}{2}R$. Answers A, B and D represent choices that students are likely to find if they do the math incorrectly.

13. B: The total energy of an isolated system is always conserved. However the mechanical energy may not be, since some mechanical energy could be converted into radiation (light) or heat (through friction). According to Einstein's famous equation $E = mc^2$, energy is (occasionally, like in nuclear reactions!) converted into mass, and vice versa, where c is the speed of light. This does not affect the conservation of energy law, however, since the mass is considered to have an energy equivalent. This equation does not tell anything about the mechanical energy of a particle; it just shows how much energy would be generated if the mass was converted directly into energy.

14. D: The phase of a wave changes as the wave moves. When measured in radians, the phase fluctuates between 0 and 2π radians. It is this fluctuating angle that allows two identical waves to be either in or out of phase, depending on whether their sinusoidal forms are matching or not when they cross. Answers A and B are meant to emulate the wave's amplitude and wavelength, both of which are measured in units of distance (meters, for example) and not radians.

15. C: Although the acceleration of a falling object is constant (9.8 m/s^2), this is not true for a pendulum. The total force on a simple pendulum is the resultant of the force of gravity on the bob acting downward and the tension in the string. When the pendulum is at the bottom of its swing, the net force is zero (tension = weight), although the bob does have a velocity. At the top of its swing, when it's changing direction, the tension is least. Therefore, the net force is greatest here, too. The bob is stationary momentarily at its highest level. Since $F = ma$, a large force means that the acceleration here is highest, too.

16. A: The amplitude of waves that cross/interfere is the sum of the instantaneous height at the point the two waves cross. In this case, one wave is at its peak amplitude A. The other wave, in a trough, is at its minimum amplitude -A. Since these waves are at opposite heights, their sum = A + -A = 0. Had the waves both been peaking, the sum would be A + A = 2A. If they had both been at a minimum, the sum would be -2A.
17. C: If the waves are 500 Hz and 504 Hz, they will have 504 - 500 = 4 beats per second. By definition, this would have a frequency of 4 Hz. This would mean 0.25 seconds between beats.

18. B: The density of a homogeneous object, liquid, or gas is its mass divided by its volume or the ratio of its mass to its volume. Density is inversely proportional to the volume and directly proportional to the mass. The ratio of the density of A to the density of B is 5:4 or 5/4. Hence, the ratio of the volume of A to the volume of B is 4:5 or 4/5. Alternatively one could solve the equation $5V_A = 4V_B$.

19. C: The pressure of water at a depth h is given by ρgh where ρ is the density of water. Here P = (1000 kg/m^3 x 9.8 m/s^2 x 14 m) = $1.37 \times 10^5 \text{ N/m}^2$. To find the force of the water on the window, multiply this pressure by the window's area. F = $\pi(1m)^2$ x $1.37 \times 10^5 \text{ N/m}^2$ = $4.3 \times 10^5 \text{ N/m}^2$.

20. D: Irrotational fluid flow consists of streamlines which describe the paths taken by the fluid elements. The streamlines don't have to be straight lines because the pipe may be curved. Answer B describes the conditions for steady flow. The image of a paddle wheel may be used to explain irrotational flow, but (1) the wheel will not turn in an irrotational fluid flow, and (2) this only works if the viscosity is zero. When there is viscosity, the speed of the fluid near the surface of the pipe is less than the speed of the fluid in the center of a pipe. Rotational flow includes vortex motion, whirlpools, and eddies.

21. B: As water freezes and becomes a solid, that heat leaves the water and the temperature of the water decreases. Water is a rare exception to the rule because it expands when it freezes. Most other substances contract when they freeze because the average distance between the atoms of the substance decreases. Water, on the other hand, forms a crystal lattice when it freezes, which causes the Hydrogen and Oxygen molecules to move slightly further away from each other due to the lattice's rigid structure. The coefficient of thermal expansion is always positive. Answer C just restates the phenomena and does not give an explanation. Answer D is true but does not explain the expansion of freezing water.

22. C: The electric field at a point in space is the force acting on a small positive test charge divided by the magnitude of the test charge. Its units are newtons per coulomb and it is a vector pointing in the direction of the force. The electric field produced by a charge distribution refers to the electric fields at each point in space. All the electric field vectors are tangent to electric field lines or electric lines of force. The electric field produced by a charge distribution can be represented by all the electric field vectors. Or, it can be represented by electric field lines. In this case, the stronger the electric field the closer together the electric field lines are. Arrows on the lines indicate the direction of the electric field. Answer D is incorrect because the field is being represented by electric field lines, not electric field vectors.

23. A: Since like charges repel and opposite charges attract, putting a dipole in an electric field would cause the dipole to orient so that its negative side will point towards the electric field's positive side. Since electric fields flow from positive towards negative, an electric field pointing from south to north could be caused by positive charges in the south and negative charges in the north. Consequently, the dipole will line up opposite to this, with the positive charge on the north side. Answer B is not correct because such an orientation would be unstable. The least disturbance would cause the dipole to flip 180°.

24. B: For a positively charged particle, you would used the right hand rule (RHR) to solve this. Since this is an electron, you can either use the left hand rule, or use the RHR and switch the direction of the inducted force. The RHR gives you the direction of a force exerted by a magnetic field on a magnetic field. Holding your right hand flat, the fingers point in the direction of the velocity of a positive charge, the palm points in the direction of the magnetic field, and the thumb points in the direction of the magnetic force. For a negative charge, the force is in the opposite direction, or downward in this case.

25. C: In a vacuum, the speed of light has nothing to do with its wavelength, frequency or color. It's a constant 3×10^8 m/s. When light travels through a medium other than a vacuum, such as glass or a prism, it slows down, and technically different colors of light travel at slightly different speeds. However, in most physics problems, you should treat all light as traveling at the same speed.

26. D: "Conventional current" -- as is typically used in physics and elsewhere -- is the flow of positive charges from the positive to negative sides of a battery. In reality, protons don't actually move through a wire. Negatively charged electrons move, so conventional current

- 66 -

really reflects the effective positive charge that's created by electrons moving in the opposite direction. Normally, the wide side of the battery represents the positive side, so conventional current would start from the wide side and move around until it reached the narrow side of the battery. Here, the batteries aren't labeled with positive or negative. However, that doesn't matter, since the batteries are oriented in opposite directions. If they had the same exact voltage, no current would flow. However, if one battery has a higher voltage than the other, the higher voltage battery would dominate the direction of current flow. Since you don't know the voltage of the batteries, you cannot determine the direction of current flow.

27. B: Since the ammeter is connected in series, it will draw current and reduce the current in the resistor. However, ammeters have a very small resistance so as to draw as little current as possible. That way, measuring the current doesn't significantly affect the amount of current traveling through a circuit. Voltmeters, on the other hand, are connected in parallel and have a high resistance.

28. C: A capacitor connected to a battery with a small internal resistance will charge up very quickly because of the high current flow. Once the potential difference on the two plates becomes equal to the emf of the battery, the electrons will stop flowing from the positive plate to the negative plate and the capacitor will be fully charged up. Connecting the capacitor to a battery with a greater emf will cause the plates to acquire a greater charge. However, the charge is directly proportional to the voltage. The capacitance is the ratio of charge to voltage and depends only on the physical characteristics of the capacitor.

29. A: The maximum current is derived from Ohm's law. I = V / R = 40 V / 20 ohms = 2 amps. However, because this is an alternating current, the instantaneous current actually fluctuates between +2 amps and -2 amps. Electrons effectively move back and forth. This means the average current is 0 amps.

30. C: The angles of incidence and refraction are defined as the angle made by the rays with a line perpendicular to the surface. The angles of incidence and refraction are given by Snell's law: $n_1 \sin \theta_1 = n_2 \sin \theta_2$. In this case, because glass has a higher index of refraction (n) than air, the angle of refraction will be smaller than the angle of incidence. Increasing the angle of incidence by 5 degrees will increase the angle of refraction, but it will still be below the original 45°. Proving this with Snell's law: 1.0 x sin (50) = 1.3 sin(θ), so Sin(θ) = 0.59 and θ = 36°.

31. C: Convex is the opposite of concave. A convex mirror bulges outward like the outside of a sphere. They always produce a small image that is right side up. These images are always virtual, also, meaning the image appears to lie behind the mirror. A convex mirror with an infinite radius of curvature is essentially a plane mirror.

32. B: If the charged object is negative, it will cause electrons in the neutral object to move away from the charged object. If the charged object is positive, it will attract electrons. In both cases, there will be an attractive force. There is also an induced repulsive force, but the repulsive force is less because the like charges are farther away. An object has a net

charge because electrons have been added to a neutral object or electrons have been removed from the atoms, ions, or molecules in the object.

33. B: Answer B correctly states the definition of a conductor. Answer C is incorrect because a current will also flow in an insulator, for example, although that current will be very low. In metals, the current flow caused by an electric field is much greater than in an insulator or semiconductor because the electrons are not bound to any particular atom, but are free to move. Answer D is incorrect because a vacuum tube is a device that electrons can flow in, butut a vacuum tube is not considered a conductor.

34. C: This is a classroom demonstration of electrostatics. The paper is initially charged by induction and is attracted to the comb. When in contact with the comb, electrons migrate from the paper to the comb and the paper acquires a positive charge. Answer B is might be true, but the transfer of electrons from the paper to the comb occurs before the transfer of electrons from the air to the comb.

35. B: The two slits cause the light beams to diffract, that is, spread out instead of travelling in a straight line. As a result there are two light beams superimposed on one another. When the two light beams constructively interfere there are bright lines, and when the two light beams destructively interfere there are dark lines. Chromatic aberration has to do blurring through a lens due to different colors of light. Doppler shift affects the wavelength of light from moving sources. Total internal reflection is 100% reflection of light at the boundary between certain materials.

36. C: The emission of light is caused by photons of a specific frequency striking gas molecules, which excites their electrons and eventually causes them to emit light. Since this light comes in very specific colors, it implies that light comes is specific quanta. The ultraviolet catastrophe refers to the frequency distribution of light emitted by a blackbody. A black body is, basically, a hot object that emits radiation in a predictable pattern. The threshold frequency refers to the photoelectric effect. The stability of atoms is a quantum phenomena, however it is only indirectly connected to the existence of light quanta.

37. C: A magnifying glass is a convex lens, just like the lens used in a telescope or microscope. For objects located beyond the focal point of the lens, the image is inverted (upside down) and real. For objects located between the focal point and the lens, the image is virtual and erect (right side up). The focal length is determined by the radii of curvature of the two lens surfaces and the index of refraction of the lens material.

38. C: In physics, systematic errors occur when comparing a theoretical value with an experimental value. The experimental value differed from the actual by 2.1 pounds, which is the systematic error. Since there is always random error, Answer A is incorrect. But random error is just that — random— so it cannot be 2.1 pound, which is systematic because it's a consistent error due to the method used to take this measurement.

39. D: All of these principles are true except Snell's Law. Snell's law is $1.0 \times \sin(\theta_{incident}) = n \times \sin(\theta_{refraction})$ for a ray striking a transparent substance from a vacuum. It is true for all rays striking a lens. However, this is not a principle used in ray diagrams. Although light is bent when it enters the lens, as Snell's Law describes, it returns to its original direction when it leaves the lens. To simplify this process, it's often best to assume that a lens is infinitely thin when solving many physics problems.

40. A: In a Zn-Cu battery, the zinc terminal has a higher concentration of electrons than the copper terminal, so there is a potential difference between the locations of the two terminals. This is a form of electrical energy brought about by the chemical interactions between the metals and the electrolyte the battery uses. Creating a circuit and causing a current to flow will transform the electrical energy into heat energy, mechanical energy, or another form of electrical energy, depending on the devices in the circuit. A generator transforms mechanical energy into electrical energy and a transformer changes the electrical properties of a form of electrical energy.

Quantitative Reasoning

1. A: The product of 0.34 and 0.06 is 0.0204. Remember to count the number of places to the right of the decimal.

2. C: Use a proportion to solve the problem. $8/6 = x/15$, $60 = 3x$, $x = 20$.

3. C: $8\% = 8/100 = 2/25$.

4. A: The correct answer is $B = 3A - 2$.

5. D: $(75 + 65 + 80 + 95 + 65)/5 = 76$.

6. B: $3\ 1/4 \times 8/18 = 13/4 \times 8/18 = 104/72 = 13/9 = 1\ 4/9$.

7. C: $400/6 = 180/x$, $400x = 1080$, $x = 2.7$. Rounded to the nearest hour, it will take her approximately 3 hours.

8. D: $7/28 = 1/4$.

9. D: $x/3 + 4 = 7$, $x/3 = 3$, $x = 9$.

10. A: If x denotes short sleeve shirt and y denotes long sleeve shirt,
$x + y = 21$ and $15x + 18y = 351$
$15 (21 - y) + 18y = 351$
$315 - 15y + 18y = 351$
$3y = 36$

y = 12 and x = 9

11. B: The cheapest cookie is $1.50, times 3 is $4.50.

12. A: $6 + $4.50 + $7.50 + $6 = $24. 10% of $24 = $2.40. $24 - $2.40 = $21.60.

13. C: 47 x 8/100 = 376/100 = 3.76.

14. C: 1 1/2 x 3 = 4 1/2.

15. B: (4 x 9) – (1/2 x 6) = 36 – 3 = 33.

16. B: The product .007 and 7.5 is 0.0525. Remember to count the number of places to the right of the decimal.

17. B: Approximately 5/7 of the year is non-weekend days. $365,000 x 5/7 = $260,714.

18. C: (175 + 320 + 417 + 533 + 210)/5 = 331.

19. A: The income ($7,056,238) minus expenses ($3,998,100) = $3,058,138.

20. D: -10 is greater than -(-(-15)), which can also be written as -15.

21. A: -4 – (-9) = -4 + 9 = 5.

22. A: 60 divided by -4 is -15.

23. C: 184,770 divided by 12,318 is 15.

24. D: 7 - 5 6/13 is 1 7/13.

25. B: T + C = 21. T = 3C + 1. If you solve for 21 – C = 3C + 1, you get 3C + C = 20. 4C = 20. C = 5.

26. A: 24/X = 60/100 = 3/5. 24 x 5 = 3X. 120 = 3X. X = 40.

27. C: 0.09356 – 0.003784 is 0.089776.

28. C: 8/X = 40/100 = 2/5. 8 x 5 = 2X. 40 = 2X. x = 20.

29. D: Remember that D = RT. 260 = 65T. T = 4.

30. B: A 20% increase in both sides gives dimensions of 24 and 36. To find the area, we multiply 24 x 36 and get 864 square inches.

31. D: 1 yard = 3 feet = 36 inches. 1 yard/36 inches= (4 1/3 yards)/X inches. X = 36 x 4 1/3. X = 36 x 13/3. X = 156.

32. C: (-4)(-2)(-6) = 8 x (-6) = -48.

33. A: Volume = LWH. Here that is 14 x 10 x 3 = 420.

34. A: The equation for finding perimeter is P = 2L + 2W. Here P = 2x300 + 2x640 = 600 + 1280 = 1880.

35. B: 2^3 + (4 + 1) = 2 x 2 x 2 + 5 = 8 + 5 = 13.

36. B: The product of 3.75 and 0.004 is 0.015. Remember to count the number of places to the right of the decimal.

37. C: 7 2/3 x 3 = 23/3 x 3 = 23.

38. A: 7 5/8 divided by 3 3/4 = 61/8 x 4/15 = 244/120 = 61/30 = 2 1/30.

39. B: The average of 7 and x is 7 + x divided by 2. The average of 9, 4, and x is 9 + 4 + x divided by 3. (7+x)/2 = (9+4+x)/3. Simplify the problem and eliminate the denominators by multiplying the first side by 3 and the second side by 2. For the first equation, (21 + 3x)/6. For the second equation, (18 + 8 + 2x)/6. Since the denominators are the same, they can be eliminated, leaving 21 + 3x = 26 + 2x. Solving for x gets x = 26-21. x = 5.

40. D: This is a simple average problem. If x denotes Annie's score, 86+98+90+x, divided by 4 equals 92. To solve, multiply each side by 4 and add the known scores together to get 274 + x = 368. Subtract 274 from 368 to solve for x. x = 94.

Practice Test 2

Natural Science

Biology

1. Which of the following metabolic compounds is composed of only carbon, oxygen, and hydrogen?
   a. Phospholipids
   b. Glycogen
   c. Peptides
   d. RNA
   e. Vitamins

2. Which of the following organelles is/are formed when the plasma membrane surrounds a particle outside of the cell?
   a. Golgi bodies
   b. Rough endoplasmic reticulum
   c. Lysosomes
   d. Secretory vesicles
   e. Endocytic vesicles

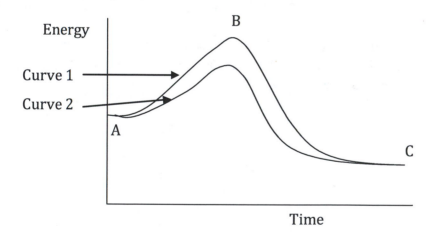

3. The graph above shows the potential energy of molecules during the process of a chemical reaction. All of the following may be true EXCEPT
   a. This is an endergonic reaction
   b. The activation energy in curve 2 is less than the activation energy in curve 1
   c. The energy of the products is less than the energy of the substrate
   d. Curve 2 shows the reaction in the presence of an enzyme
   e. The reaction required ATP

4. How many chromosomes does a human cell have after meiosis I?
   a. 92
   b. 46
   c. 23
   d. 22
   e. 12

5. A length of DNA coding for a particular protein is called a(n)
   a. Allele
   b. Genome
   c. Gene
   d. Transcript
   e. Codon

6. Which type of plant produces seeds that are housed inside a fruit
   a. Monocots
   b. Dicots
   c. Angiosperms
   d. Gymnosperms
   e. Nonvascular plants

7. Which of the following is an example of the alternation of generations life cycle?
   a. Asexual reproduction of strawberries by runners
   b. Annual plants that live through a single growing season
   c. Ferns that have a large diploid and a diminutive haploid stage
   d. Insects that have distinct larval and adult stages
   e. Reptiles that have long periods of dormancy and metabolic inactivity

8. Animals exchange gases with the environment in all of the following ways EXCEPT
   a. Direct exchange through the skin
   b. Exchange through gills
   c. Stomata
   d. Tracheae
   e. Lungs

9. Which of the following blood components is involved in blood clotting?
   a. Red blood cells
   b. Platelets
   c. White blood cells
   d. Leukocytes
   e. Plasma

10. Which hormone is *not* secreted by a gland in the brain?
   a. Human chorionic gonadotropin (HCG)
   b. Gonadotropin releasing hormone (GnRH)
   c. Luteinizing hormone (LH)
   d. Follicle stimulating hormone (FSH)
   e. None of these

11. Which of the following is true of the gastrula?
   a. It is a solid ball of cells
   b. It has three germ layers
   c. It is an extraembryonic membrane
   d. It gives rise to the blastula
   e. It derives from the zona pellucida

12. Which of the following is the major way in which carbon is released into the environment?
   a. Transpiration
   b. Respiration
   c. Fixation
   d. Sedimentation
   e. Absorption

13. During primary succession, which species would most likely be a pioneer species?
   a. Lichens
   b. Fir trees
   c. Mosquitoes
   d. Dragonflies
   e. Mushrooms

14. Two species of finches are able to utilize the same food supply, but their beaks are different. They are able to coexist on an island because of
   a. Niche overlap
   b. Character displacement
   c. Resource partitioning
   d. Competitive exclusion
   e. Realized niches

15. Which of the following processes of speciation would most likely occur if a species of bird were introduced into a group of islands that were previously uninhabited by animals?
   a. Allopatric speciation
   b. Adaptive radiation
   c. Sympatric speciation
   d. Artificial speciation
   e. Hybridizing speciation

16. The first living cells on earth were most likely
    a. Heterotrophs
    b. Autotrophs
    c. Aerobic
    d. Eukaryotes
    e. Photosynthetic

17. Which of the following is not a function of protein in a cell?
    a. Encoding genetic information
    b. Storage of energy
    c. Structural support
    d. Transport of materials
    e. Catalysis of chemical reactions

18. Biochemical reactions take place in an enzyme's?
    a. Cofactor site
    b. Active site
    c. Prosthetic group
    d. Substrate complex
    e. Endothermic site

19. Cyanide is a poison that binds to the active site of the enzyme cytochrome c and prevents its activity. This kind of inhibition is called:
    a. Feedback inhibition
    b. Allosteric inhibition
    c. Competitive inhibition
    d. Noncompetitive inhibition
    e. Cooperativity

20. Which of the following is a characteristic of enzymes?
    a. They often catalyze more than one kind of reaction
    b. They are sensitive to denaturation by heat
    c. They catalyze reactions in only one direction
    d. They are primarily regulated by gene transcription
    e. They all require ATP

21. Which of the following photosynthetic reactions can only take place in the presence of light?
    a. Chemosmosis
    b. Photorespiration
    c. The Calvin Cycle
    d. Carbon fixation
    e. C4 photosynthesis

22. Which of the following would be most disruptive to the flowering time of a short-day plant?
   a. Daylight interrupted by a brief dark period
   b. Daylight interrupted by a long dark period
   c. High daytime temperatures
   d. Watering only at night
   e. Night interrupted by a brief exposure to red light

23. The digestion of starches begins in which part of the digestive system?
   a. The mouth
   b. The stomach
   c. The small intestine
   d. The large intestine
   e. The colon

24. Which of the following would NOT be an effective strategy for thermoregulation in a hot environment?
   a. Evaporation of water from the skin surface
   b. Restricting activity to nights
   c. Countercurrent exchange
   d. Increasing blood flow to extremities
   e. Muscle contraction

25. Two alleles of a gene will have the same
   a. Dominance
   b. Phenotypes
   c. Frequency in a population
   d. Locus
   e. Penetrance

26. In fruit flies, the traits for abdomen bristles and wing shape have several alleles but are always inherited together. This is an example of:
   a. Epistasis
   b. Pleiotropy
   c. Linkage
   d. Polygenic inheritance
   e. Incomplete dominance

27. Which of the following is the best example of a K-selected species?
   a. Grasses
   b. Mosquitoes
   c. Gorillas
   d. Mice
   e. Beetles

28. Which of the following is an example of a density-independent limiting factor?
    a. Sunlight for photosynthesis
    b. Food availability
    c. Predation
    d. Transmission of infectious diseases
    e. Pollution

29. Which of the following is *least* likely to cause a change in allele frequencies in a population?
    a. Mutation
    b. Random mating
    c. Immigration
    d. A rapid decrease in population size due to a natural disaster
    e. Inbreeding

30. Which of the following conditions would most likely lead to adaptive radiation?
    a. A mountain rising up and creating two separate populations of a species
    b. A plant becoming polyploid
    c. Hybridization between two species of flowers
    d. Inbreeding among a population
    e. Introduction of an animal onto a previously uncolonized island

31. Evidence that eukaryotic organelles evolved from prokaryotes includes all of the following EXCEPT:
    a. Mitochondria and chloroplasts have their own DNA
    b. Fossils of early endosymbionts
    c. Mitochondria and chloroplasts have two membranes
    d. Mitochondria and chloroplasts reproduce independently of the cell cycle
    e. Internal organelles are similar in size to prokaryotes

32. Which of the following chemical moieties forms the backbone of DNA?
    a. Nitrogenous bases
    b. Glycerol
    c. Amino groups
    d. Pentose and phosphate
    e. Glucose and phosphate

33. Which enzyme in DNA replication is a potential source of new mutations?
    a. DNA ligase
    b. Primase
    c. DNA gyrase
    d. DNA polymerase
    e. Topoisomerase

34. The *lac* operon controls
    a. Conjugation between bacteria
    b. Chromatin organization
    c. Gene transcription
    d. Excision repair
    e. Termination of translation

35. A bacterial mini-chromosome used in recombinant DNA technology is called a
    a. Centromere
    b. Telomere
    c. Plasmid
    d. Transposon
    e. cDNA

36. DNA and RNA are similar in which of the following ways?
    a. Both contain the sugar ribose
    b. Both grow in the $5' \rightarrow 3'$ direction during replication or transcription
    c. Both are usually double-stranded
    d. Both contain the base thymine
    e. Both can serve as a template for translation

37. An embryo directly maintains pregnancy by secreting which hormone?
    a. Human chorionic gonadotropin (HCG)
    b. Gonadotropin releasing hormone (GnRH)
    c. Luteinizing hormone (LH)
    d. Follicle stimulating hormone (FSH)
    e. None of these

38. Which of the following structures contains the genetic material in sperm?
    a. The acrosome
    b. The midpiece
    c. The tail
    d. The flagellum
    e. The head

39. If non-disjunction occurs in a late stage of embryonic development, the result will be
    a. Polyploidy
    b. Down syndrome
    c. Mosaicism
    d. Turner syndrome
    e. Deletion

40. A child is born with the O blood type. His mother is type O and his father is type A. What are the genotypes of his mother and father?
   a. IAIA and ii
   b. ii and IAi
   c. IA i and IA i
   d. IAi and IBi
   e. ii and ii

General Chemistry

1. A gas at constant volume is cooled. Which statement about the gas must be true?
   a. The kinetic energy of the gas molecules has decreased.
   b. The gas has condensed to a liquid.
   c. The weight of the gas has decreased.
   d. The density of the gas has increased.

2. Graham's law is best used to determine what relationship between two different materials?
   a. pressure and volume
   b. volume and temperature
   c. mass and diffusion rate
   d. Diffusion rate and temperature

3. A 10 L cylinder contains 4 moles of oxygen, 3 moles of nitrogen and 7 moles of neon. The temperature of the cylinder is increased from 20 °C to 40 °C. Determine the partial pressure of neon in the cylinder as a percentage of the whole.
   a. 50%
   b. 70%
   c. 90%
   d. 40%

4. Which of the following statements **generally** describes the trend of electronegativity considering the Periodic Table of the Elements?
   a. Electronegativity increases going from left to right and from top to bottom
   b. Electronegativity increases going from right to left and from bottom to top
   c. Electronegativity increases going from left to right and from bottom to top
   d. Electronegativity increases going from right to left and from top to bottom

5. A solid is heated until it melts. Which of the following is true about the solid melting?
   a. ΔH is positive, and ΔS is positive
   b. ΔH is negative and ΔS is positive
   c. ΔH is positive and ΔS is negative
   d. ΔH is negative and ΔS is negative

6. 100 g of ethanol C_2H_6O is dissolved in 100 g of water. The final solution has a volume of 0.2 L. What is the density of the resulting solution?
   a. 0.5 g/mL
   b. 1 g/mL
   c. 46 g/mL
   d. 40 g/mL

7. Place the following in the correct order of increasing acidity.
   a. HCl<HF<HI<HBr
   b. HCl<HBr<HI<HF
   c. HI<HBr<HCl<HF
   d. HF<HCl<HBr<HI

8. Ammonium Phosphate $(NH_4)_3PO_4$ is a strong electrolyte. What will be the concentration of all the ions in a 0.9 M solution of ammonium phosphate?
   a. 0.9 M NH_4+, 0.9 M PO_4^{3-}
   b. 0.3 M NH_4+, 0.9 M PO_4^{3-}
   c. 2.7 M NH_4+, 0.9 M PO_4^{3-}
   d. 2.7 M NH_4^+, 2.7 M PO_4^{3-}

9. A 1 M solution of NaCl (A) and a 0.5 M solution of NaCl (B) are joined together by a semi permeable membrane. What, if anything, is likely to happen between the two solutions?
   a. No change, the solvents and solutes are the same in each
   b. Water will migrate from A to B
   c. NaCl will migrate from A to B and water will migrate from B to A.
   d. Water will migrate from B to A.

10. C-14 has a half life of 5730 years. If you started with 1 mg of C-14 today, how much would be left in 20,000 years?
   a. 0.06 mg
   b. 0.07 mg
   c. 0.11 mg
   d. 0.09 mg

11. Determine the number of neutrons, protons and electrons in ^{238}U.
   a. 238, 92, 238
   b. 92, 146, 146
   c. 146, 92, 92
   d. 92, 92, 146

12. Determine the oxidation states of each of the elements in $KMnO_4$:
   a. K^{+1}, Mn^{+7}, O^{-8}
   b. K^{-1}, Mn^{+7}, O^{-2}
   c. K^{+1}, Mn^{+3}, O^{-4}
   d. K^{+1}, Mn^{+7}, O^{-2}

13. Which of the following is an incorrect Lewis structure?

I. (structure) II. (structure) III. $: \ddot{Br}-\ddot{Br} :$ IV. $CH_3-\ddot{Cl} :$

   a. I
   b. II
   c. III
   d. IV

14. What is the correct IUPAC name of the compound Fe_2O_3?
   a. Iron (I) oxide
   b. Iron (II) oxide
   c. Iron (III) oxide
   d. Iron (IV) oxide

15. Magnesium metal is reacted with hydrobromic acid according to the following equation:

$$Mg + 2HBr \rightarrow MgBr_2 + H_2$$

If 100 g of Mg is reacted with 100 g of HBr, which statement about the reaction is true?
   a. Mg is the limiting reagent
   b. HBr is the excess reagent
   c. Mg is the excess reagent
   d. 100 g of $MgBr_2$ will be produced

16. For the gas phase reaction $CH_4 + 4Cl_2 \rightarrow CCl_4 + 4HCl$, what would be the equilibrium expression K_{eq} for this reaction?
   a. $[CH_4][Cl_2] / [CCl_4][4HCl]$
   b. $[CH_4][Cl_2] / [CCl_4][HCl]^4$
   c. $[4Cl][CCl_4\} / [CH_4][4HCl]$
   d. $[CCl_4][HCl]^4 / [CH_4][Cl_2]^4$

17. The pka for ethanol (CH_3CH_2OH) is approximately 16. The pka for acetic acid (CH_3COOH) is about 4. The difference can be explained by:
   a. Resonance stabilization
   b. Electronegativity differences
   c. Molecular weight differences
   d. Molecular size differences

18. 50 mL of 1 M H_2SO_4 is added to an aqueous solution containing 4 g of NaOH. What will the final pH of the resulting solution be?
   a. 5
   b. 6
   c. 7
   d. 9

19. Which of the following reactions produces products with higher entropy than the starting materials?

I. Glucose (s) + water →glucose (aq)

II. 4Al (s) + 3O$_2$(g)→2Al$_2$O$_3$(s)

III. Br$_2$ + light→2 Br

IV. Ice →water vapor

a. II, III
b. I, II
c. I, III
d. I, III, IV

20. Which of the following molecules is named correctly?

A.

methyl propionoate

B.   OH

1-propanol

C.

3-propanoic acid

D.

3-butene

21. What would be the best analytical tool for determining the chemical structure of an organic compound?

a. NMR
b. HPLC
c. IR
d. Mass spec

22. The transformation of diamond to graphite has a −ΔG. Which of the following is true?

a. The reaction is spontaneous and occurs rapidly at room temperature
b. The reaction is not spontaneous and occurs slowly at room temperature
c. The reaction is not spontaneous and does not occur at room temperature
d. The reaction is spontaneous and occurs slowly at room temperature

23. What is the oxidation state of the carbon atom in a carboxylic acid functional group?

a. 4+
b. 3+
c. 2-
d. 3-

24. Which scientist was responsible for developing the format of the modern periodic table?
    a. Faraday
    b. Einstein
    c. Hess
    d. Mendeleev

25. Two different molecules can be isomers of each other if:
    a. They have the same functional groups
    b. They have the same oxidation state
    c. They have the same molecular weight
    d. They have the same chemical formula

26. Proteins are made up of which of the following repeating subunits?
    a. Sugars
    b. Triglycerides
    c. Amino acids
    d. Nucleic acids

27. 100 g of H_3PO_4 is dissolved in water, producing 400 mL of solution. What is the normality of the solution?
    a. 2.55 N
    b. 1.02 N
    c. 7.65 N
    d. 0.25 N

28. Which statement about the impact of chemistry on society is not true?
    a. Fluoridation of water has had no effect on the rate of cavities as compared to unfluoridated water
    b. Chemical fertilizers have tremendously increased food production per acre in the U.S.
    c. Chemistry played a central role in the development of nuclear weapons
    d. Use of catalytic converters in automobiles has greatly reduced acid rain producing exhaust products

29. The density of a material refers to:
    a. Mass per volume
    b. Mass per mole
    c. Molecular weight per volume
    d. Moles per volume

30. Which of the following types of chemicals are considered generally unsafe to store together?

I. Liquids and solids
II. Acids and bases
III. Reducing agents and oxidizing agents
IV. Metals and salts

    a. I, II
    b. II, III
    c. III, IV
    d. I, IV

Organic Chemistry

1. A compound with the molecular formula $C_6H_{14}O$ is
    a. an alcohol or an ether
    b. an aldehyde or a ketone
    c. an alcohol or an aldehyde
    d. an ether or a ketone

2. Which structure is a possible representation of the molecular formula C_6H_6?

a.
                  c.

b.
                  d.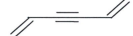

3. 1-Methylcyclohexene reacts with strong aqueous acid to produce
    a. no reaction occurs
    b. 1-methylcyclohexanol
    c. 2-methylcyclohexanol
    d. cyclohexylmethanol

4. A carbon atom and an oxygen atom double-bonded to each other is called
    a. a carbonyl group
    b. a carbonate group
    c. a carboxylic function
    d. an acyl group

5. Optical isomerism occurs in compounds that
    a. are enantiomeric
    b. are symmetric
    c. have multiple isomers
    d. have only one isomer

6. A molecular structure that is not superimposable with its mirror image isomer is called
    a. a geometric isomer
    b. a conformational isomer
    c. an enantiomeric isomer
    d. a structural isomer

7. Multiple bonds between atoms are characterized by
    a. shorter bond lengths and higher bond energies
    b. lower bond energies and shorter bond lengths
    c. decreased reactivity
    d. increased molecular weight

8. Chromatography is
    a. a method of separating and purifying compounds in a mixture
    b. an aid to identifying compounds in a mixture
    c. both a) and b) are true
    d. neither a) nor b) are true

9. The following molecule is

    a. a conjugated enone
    b. 2-phenyl-5-methylhept-4-en-2-one
    c. 2-cyclohexyl-2,5-dimethylhex-4-en-3-one
    d. known as caffeine

10. The IR spectrum of a compound has a strong, sharp absorption band at 1786 cm^{-1}, indicating the presence of
    a. a C=O bond
    b. a C≡N bond
    c. an ether C-O-C linkage
    d. a C=C bond

11. The reaction between a secondary alkyl bromide and hydroxide to produce a secondary alcohol normally proceeds via
    a. an S_N1 reaction mechanism
    b. an S_N2 reaction mechanism
    c. an E1 reaction mechanism
    d. an E2 reaction mechanism

12. Chromatography is a method of purifying compounds that depends on
    a. solubility
    b. absorption
    c. adsorption/desorption equilibria
    d. polarity

13. Six-carbon and five-carbon sugars
    a. have cyclic and acyclic forms
    b. are bicyclic
    c. cannot bond together
    d. cannot be recrystallized

14. When Mg metal is added to a solution of 1-bromopropane in diethyl ether
    a. a Grignard reaction takes place
    b. a Grignard reagent is formed
    c. no reaction occurs
    d. $MgBr_2$ is formed

15. The Grignard reaction between isobutyl magnesium bromide and cyclohexanone in anhydrous diethyl ether produces
    a. 1-(2-methylpropyl)-cyclohexanol
    b. cyclohexyl 2-methylpropyl ether
    c. 1-bromocyclohexanol
    d. cyclohexyl 2-methylpropanoate

16. The reaction of phenylacetyl chloride with toluene and ferric chloride produces
    a. p-(phenylacetyl)toluene
    b. phenylmethyl p-tolyl ketone
    c. 1-(2-phenylacetyl)-4-methyl benzene
    d. all of the above

17. The geometry of the amide functional group in amides is
    a. trigonal planar due to p orbital overlap
    b. tetrahedral at the N atom
    c. unaffected by the lone pair orbital on the N atom
    d. subject to free rotation about the C-N bond

18. The Wittig reaction involves
    a. addition of a phosphine to an imine
    b. addition of a phosphinium ylide to a carbonyl group
    c. addition of a phosphine oxide to a carbonyl group
    d. none of the above

19. The Williamson synthesis can be used to produce
    a. alcohols from ethers
    b. ethers from alcohols
    c. furanose saccharides from alcohols
    d. cyclic amines from alcohols

20. The steroid nucleus is

a)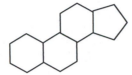

c)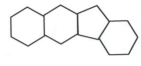

b)

d) C'

21. A reaction in which two additional ring structures are added to a substrate molecule in the same reaction is called
    a. an annulation reaction
    b. a bicycloannulation reaction
    c. a double addition reaction
    d. a coordination reaction

22. Which of the following pairs of compounds are nitrogen heterocycles?
    a. maleimide and imidazole
    b. pyridine and piperidine
    c. caffeine and ☐-butyrolactam
    d. all of the above

23. Bonds between nitrogen and oxygen are found in
    a. amine oxides and oximes
    b. cyanates and isocyanates
    c. pyrans and furans
    d. imines and epoxides

24. Acid hydrolysis of nitriles can be used to form
    a. alcohols
    b. amines
    c. nitrates
    d. amides

25. The glass transition temperature of a polymer is
    a. the temperature at which the material becomes glass-like when heated
    b. the temperature at which the material becomes not glass-like when heated
    c. the temperature at which the material shatters when heated
    d. none of the above

26. Saponification of the triglycerides trimyristin and tristearin ultimately produces
    a. myristic acid and stearic acid
    b. myristine and stearine
    c. myristine and stearic acid
    d. myristic acid, stearic acid, and glycerol

27. Diols and glycerol react with dicarboxylic acids to form
    a. linear and cross-linked polyesters
    b. diglycerides and triglycerides
    c. saccharides
    d. polyethers

28. Large unreactive molecules such as di-isooctyl terephthallate, used to add flexibility to polymers, are called
    a. adjuvants
    b. block copolymers
    c. stabilizers
    d. plasticizers

29. Starches and celluloses are constructed by the polymerization of
    a. fructose molecules
    b. galactose molecules
    c. glucose molecules
    d. galactulose molecules

30. A polymer that softens when heated is said to be
    a. thermonuclear
    b. thermosetting
    c. thermoplastic
    d. neoplastic

Reading Comprehension

Questions 1 – 5 are based on the following passage:

Usher syndrome is the most common condition that affects both hearing and vision. The major symptoms of Usher syndrome are hearing loss and an eye disorder called retinitis pigmentosa, or RP. Retinitis pigmentosa causes night blindness and a loss of peripheral vision (side vision) through the progressive degeneration of the retina. The retina, which is crucial for vision, is a light-sensitive tissue at the back of the eye. As RP progresses, the field of vision narrows, until only central vision (the ability to see straight ahead) remains. Many people with Usher syndrome also have severe balance problems.

There are three clinical types of Usher syndrome. In the United States, types 1 and 2 are the most common. Together, they account for approximately 90 to 95 percent of all cases of juvenile Usher syndrome. Approximately three to six percent of all deaf and hearing-disabled children have Usher syndrome. In developed countries, such as the United States, about four in every 100,000 newborns have Usher syndrome.

Usher syndrome is inherited as an autosomal recessive trait. The term autosomal means that the mutated gene is not located on either of the chromosomes that determine sex; in other words, both males and females can have the disorder and can pass it along to a child. The word recessive means that in order to have Usher syndrome, an individual must receive a mutated form of the Usher syndrome gene from each parent. If a child has a mutation in one Usher syndrome gene but the other gene is normal, he or she should have normal vision and hearing. Individuals with a mutation in a gene that can cause an autosomal recessive disorder are called carriers, because they carry the mutated gene but show no symptoms of the disorder. If both parents are carriers of a mutated gene for Usher syndrome, they will have a one-in-four chance of producing a child with Usher syndrome.

Usually, parents who have normal hearing and vision do not know if they are carriers of an Usher syndrome gene mutation. Currently, it is not possible to determine whether an individual without a family history of Usher syndrome is a carrier. Scientists at the National Institute on Deafness and Other Communication Disorders (NIDCD) are hoping to change this, however, as they learn more about the genes responsible for Usher syndrome.

1. What is the main idea of the passage?
   a. Usher syndrome is an inherited condition that affects hearing and vision.
   b. Some people are carriers of Usher syndrome.
   c. Usher syndrome typically skips a generation.
   d. Scientists hope to develop a test for detecting the carriers of Usher syndrome.

2. What is the meaning of the word *symptoms* as it is used in the first paragraph?
   a. qualifications
   b. conditions
   c. disorders
   d. perceptible signs

3. Which statement is *not* a detail from the passage?
   a. Types 1 and 2 Usher syndrome are the most common in the United States.
   b. Usher syndrome affects both hearing and smell.
   c. Right now, there is no way to identify a carrier of Usher syndrome.
   d. Central vision is the ability to see straight ahead.

4. What is the meaning of the word *juvenile* as it is used in the second paragraph?
   a. bratty
   b. serious
   c. occurring in children
   d. improper

5. What is the meaning of the word *mutated* as it is used in the third paragraph?
   a. selected
   b. altered
   c. composed
   d. destroyed

Questions 6 – 9 are based on the following passage:

Anemia is a condition in which there is an abnormally low number of red blood cells (RBCs). This condition also can occur if the RBCs don't contain enough hemoglobin, the iron-rich protein that makes the blood red. Hemoglobin helps RBCs carry oxygen from the lungs to the rest of the body.

Anemia can be accompanied by low numbers of RBCs, white blood cells (WBCs), and platelets. Red blood cells are disc-shaped and look like doughnuts without holes in the center. They carry oxygen and remove carbon dioxide (a waste product) from your body. These cells are made in the bone marrow and live for about 120 days in the bloodstream. Platelets and WBCs also are made in the bone marrow. White blood cells help fight infection. Platelets stick together to seal small cuts or breaks on the blood vessel walls and to stop bleeding.

If you are anemic, your body doesn't get enough oxygenated blood. As a result, you may feel tired or have other symptoms. Severe or long-lasting anemia can damage the heart, brain, and other organs of the body. Very severe anemia may even cause death.

Anemia has three main causes: blood loss, lack of RBC production, or high rates of RBC destruction. Many types of anemia are mild, brief, and easily treated. Some types can be prevented with a healthy diet or treated with dietary supplements. However, certain types of anemia may be severe, long lasting, and life threatening if not diagnosed and treated.

If you have the signs or symptoms of anemia, you should see your doctor to find out whether you have the condition. Treatment will depend on the cause and severity of the anemia.

6. What is the main idea of the passage?
   a. Anemia presents in a number of forms.
   b. Anemia is a potentially dangerous condition characterized by low numbers of RBCs.
   c. Anemia is a deficiency of WBCs and platelets.
   d. Anemia is a treatable condition.

7. Which statement is *not* a detail from the passage?
   a. There are different methods for treating anemia.
   b. Red blood cells remove carbon dioxide from the body.
   c. Platelets are made in the bone marrow.
   d. Anemia is rarely caused by blood loss.

8. What is the meaning of the word *oxygenated* as it is used in the third paragraph?
   a. containing low amounts of oxygen
   b. containing no oxygen
   c. consisting entirely of oxygen
   d. containing high amounts of oxygen

9. What is the meaning of the word *severity* as it is used in the fifth paragraph?
   a. seriousness
   b. disconnectedness
   c. truth
   d. swiftness

Questions 10 – 13 are based on the following passage:

Contrary to previous reports, drinking four or more cups of coffee a day does not put women at risk of rheumatoid arthritis (RA), according to a new study partially funded by the National Institute of Arthritis and Musculoskeletal and Skin Diseases (NIAMS). The study concluded that there is little evidence to support a connection between consuming coffee or tea and the risk of RA among women.

Rheumatoid arthritis is an inflammatory autoimmune disease that affects the joints. It results in pain, stiffness, swelling, joint damage, and loss of function. Inflammation most often affects the hands and feet and tends to be symmetrical. About one percent of the U.S. population has rheumatoid arthritis.

Elizabeth W. Karlson, M.D., and her colleagues at Harvard Medical School and Brigham and Women's Hospital in Boston, Massachusetts, used the Nurses' Health Study, a long-term investigation of nurses' diseases, lifestyles, and health practices, to examine possible links between caffeinated beverages and RA risk. The researchers were able to follow up more than 90 percent of the original pool of 83,124 participants who answered a 1980 food frequency questionnaire, and no links were found. They also considered changes in diet and habits over a prolonged period of time, and when the results were adjusted for other factors, such as cigarette smoking, alcohol consumption, and oral contraceptive use, the outcome still showed no relationship between caffeine consumption and risk of RA.

Previous research had suggested an association between consuming coffee or tea and RA risk. According to Dr. Karlson, the data supporting that conclusion were inconsistent. Because the information in the older studies was collected at only one time, she says, consideration was not given to the other factors associated with RA, such as cigarette smoking and changes in diet and lifestyle over a follow-up period. The new study presents a more accurate picture of caffeine and RA risk.

10. What is the main idea of the passage?
    a. In the past, doctors have cautioned older women to avoid caffeinated beverages.
    b. Rheumatoid arthritis affects the joints of older women.
    c. A recent study found no link between caffeine consumption and RA among women.
    d. Cigarette smoking increases the incidence of RA.

11. Which statement is *not* a detail from the passage?
    a. Alcohol consumption is linked with RA.
    b. The original data for the study came from a 1980 questionnaire.
    c. Rheumatoid arthritis most often affects the hands and feet.
    d. This study included tens of thousands of participants.

12. What is the meaning of the word *symmetrical* as it is used in the second paragraph?
    a. affecting both sides of the body in corresponding fashion
    b. impossible to treat
    c. sensitive to the touch
    d. asymptomatic

13. What is the author's primary purpose in writing the essay?
    a. to entertain
    b. to inform
    c. to analyze
    d. to persuade

Questions 14 – 17 are based on the following passage:
    Exercise is vital at every age for healthy bones. Not only does exercise improve bone health, but it also increases muscle strength, coordination, and balance, and it leads to better overall health. Exercise is especially important for preventing and treating osteoporosis.

Like muscle, bone is living tissue that responds to exercise by becoming stronger. Young women and men who exercise regularly generally achieve greater peak bone mass (maximum bone density and strength) than those who do not. For most people, bone mass peaks during the third decade of life. After that time, we can begin to lose bone. Women and men older than age 20 can help prevent bone loss with regular exercise. Exercise maintains muscle strength, coordination, and balance, which in turn prevent falls and related fractures. This is especially important for older adults and people with osteoporosis.

Weight-bearing exercise is the best kind of exercise for bones, which forces the muscle to work against gravity. Some examples of weight-bearing exercises are weight training, walking, hiking, jogging, climbing stairs, tennis, and dancing. Swimming and bicycling, on the other hand, are not weight-bearing exercises. Although these activities help build and maintain strong muscles and have excellent cardiovascular benefits, they are not the best exercise for bones.

14. What is the main idea of the passage?
    a. Weight-bearing exercise is the best for bones.
    b. Exercise increases balance.
    c. Exercise improves bone health.
    d. Women benefit from regular exercise more than men.

15. What is the meaning of the word *vital* as it is used in the first paragraph?
    a. deadly
    b. important
    c. rejected
    d. nourishing

16. Which statement is *not* a detail from the passage?
    a. Tennis is a form of weight-bearing exercise.
    b. Most people reach peak bone mass in their twenties.
    c. Swimming is not good for the bones.
    d. Bone is a living tissue.

17. What is the meaning of the word *fractures* as it is used in the second paragraph?
    a. breaks
    b. agreements
    c. tiffs
    d. fevers

Questions 18 – 21 are based on the following passage:

Searching for medical information can be confusing, especially for first-timers. However, if you are patient and stick to it, you can find a wealth of information. Your community library is a good place to start your search for medical information. Before going to the library, you may find it helpful to make a list of topics you want information about and questions you have. Your list of topics and questions will make it easier for the librarian to direct you to the best resources.

Many community libraries have a collection of basic medical references. These references may include medical dictionaries or encyclopedias, drug information handbooks, basic medical and nursing textbooks, and directories of physicians and medical specialists (listings of doctors). You may also find magazine articles on a certain topic. Look in the Reader's Guide to Periodical Literature for articles on health and medicine from consumer magazines.

Infotrac, a CD-ROM computer database available at libraries or on the Web, indexes hundreds of popular magazines and newspapers, as well as medical journals such as the Journal of the American Medical Association and New England Journal of Medicine. Your library may also carry searchable computer databases of medical journal articles, including MEDLINE/PubMed or the Cumulative Index to Nursing and Allied Health Literature. Many of the databases or indexes have abstracts that provide a summary of each journal article. Although most community libraries don't have a large collection of medical and nursing journals, your librarian may be able to get copies of the articles you want. Interlibrary loans allow your librarian to request a copy of an article from a library that carries that particular medical journal. Your library may charge a fee for this service. Articles published in medical journals can be technical, but they may be the most current source of information on medical topics.

18. What is the main idea of the passage?
   a. Infotrac is a useful source of information.
   b. The community library offers numerous resources for medical information.
   c. Searching for medical information can be confusing.
   d. There is no reason to prepare a list of topics before visiting the library.

19. What is the meaning of the word *popular* as it is used in the third paragraph?
   a. complicated
   b. old-fashioned
   c. beloved
   d. for the general public

20. Which statement is *not* a detail from the passage?
   a. Abstracts summarize the information in an article.
   b. Having a prepared list of questions enables the librarian to serve you better.
   c. Infotrac is a database on CD-ROM.
   d. The articles in popular magazines can be hard to understand.

21. What is the meaning of the word *technical* as it is used in the fourth paragraph?
    a. requiring expert knowledge
    b. incomplete
    c. foreign
    d. plagiarized

Questions 22 – 32 are based on the following passages:

Passage 1

One of the major challenges facing the renewable fuel industry is the variability in the pricing of traditional fossil fuels such as petroleum and coal. Those seeking to develop alternative energy sources such as wind and solar power and, especially, electric cars face an uncertain marketplace in which the price of their chief competitors, gasoline and oil, is virtually impossible to predict. This makes investing in renewable alternatives a risky business: at what price must alternative fuels be offered in order to gain a share of the market? Government can stabilize this situation – and encourage the development of green energy sources – by taxing petroleum-based fuels to establish a minimum price at the pump.

Recently, we have seen the price of gasoline, and of other fossil fuels, driven to new highs. This price increase has been driven by increasing demand, as millions of consumers in places like China and India have increased their buying power and joined Americans and Europeans behind the steering wheels of automobiles. The price of a barrel of oil has risen, creating a favorable investing environment for the development of green alternatives like electric cars. But, although the long-term trend for the price of oil is definitely upwards, it seems that every time the price peaks something happens to drive it back down. This might be an economic recession that reduces demand, a release of stockpiled oil by the government to increase supply, or simply a price manipulation by the oil companies themselves. Whatever the cause, these price reductions sour the picture for companies working on renewable energy sources, and their research and development programs often falter and stop. What can be done to forestall this boom-and-bust cycle and provide a stable investing environment to encourage the development of renewable energy?

One possibility is to use the government's power of taxation to establish a minimum price for gasoline at the pump. Under such a scheme, a variable excise tax would be triggered whenever the price of gasoline were to fall below a minimum amount, for example $3 a gallon. The amount of this tax would vary, so as to keep the price at the minimum, and the proceeds could be returned to consumers by reducing the overall income tax, or by providing tax credits to those who would be most impacted by the higher gasoline price: truck and taxi drivers, or businesses involved in the delivery of various products. And, with a stable price at the pump, companies developing electric and hybrid vehicles would be encouraged to continue their efforts with a clear view of potential profits ahead.

Passage 2

Various proposals have been put forth to encourage the development of renewable energy sources, especially in the realm of transportation, where fossil fuel-burning cars release damaging pollutants into the atmosphere while rendering the country increasingly dependent on foreign suppliers. Recently, demand from emerging economies in India, China, and even Latin America has driven the price of gasoline to new highs, adding another reason to encourage the development of alternative energy sources. Consumers are suffering from high energy prices, and they are asking, "What can the government do to keep prices under control while protecting the environment?"

We would all love to see the advent of the electric car, or of an auto that burns U.S.-produced ethanol without producing any environmental pollutants. But development has been slow. Small companies with novel approaches spring up whenever the price of oil goes up, but they seem to falter whenever it comes back down. And the major car companies, with few exceptions, have not placed a sustained effort behind the development of vehicles that burn alternatives to oil. Indeed, American car companies seem to fill their showrooms with gas-guzzlers, and their investments in electric or hybrid vehicles have not sufficed to move these programs forward rapidly. It seems that we need a policy that can encourage American ingenuity to develop forms of transportation, be they fuels or vehicles, while providing the American consumer with affordable pricing at the pump.

The government can do this without interfering with the working of the free market. After all, free market capitalism has been the driving force for innovation in this country since its inception. Any form of price manipulation, however laudable its goals, tends to have the opposite effect of that intended. Fortunately, government has at its disposal a powerful tool to encourage innovation without directly interfering in the market.

This tool is the tax credit. Tax credits reduce the amount of tax that companies have to pay on their profits, in exchange for their investments in new technologies. By providing tax credits to companies that invest in the development of electric vehicles, alternative fuels, or other forms of green energy, government could encourage the development of those products without overtly interfering in the marketplace. Consumers would ultimately benefit from a greater choice of transportation and fuel alternatives, and the goal of developing environmentally clean energy sources would be served.

22. The authors of both passages are in agreement that
   a. taxes should be used to reduce the use of oil.
   b. businesses working on renewable energy should get a tax break.
   c. a tax strategy should be used to encourage development of renewable energy sources.
   d. prices of traditional fossil fuels should be kept high.
   e. fuel prices should be manipulated.

23. A main point of disagreement between the two authors is whether or not
    a. demand from China is driving up fuel prices.
    b. consumers should be protected from high fuel prices.
    c. it is desirable to develop an electric car.
    d. high fuel prices should be maintained at the pump.
    e. companies providing renewable energy should make a profit.

24. The author of Passage 2 would probably consider the proposal in Passage 1 as
    a. another good way to help develop renewable energy sources.
    b. interference in the free market that is unlikely to succeed.
    c. useful only for developing electric cars and not for meeting other energy needs.
    d. an example of why tax policies are never a good way of guiding an industry.
    e. something that would work together with his own proposal.

25. "sour the picture" most nearly means
    a. manipulate prices
    b. lower fuel prices
    c. increase profits from existing fuels
    d. cause irate consumers to deface walls
    e. make future profits seem less likely

26. The purpose of the first paragraph in Passage 1 is to
    a. complain about low prices.
    b. establish that electric cars are good for the environment.
    c. introduce a proposal.
    d. show that companies developing new technologies must be able to expect a profit.
    e. give a detailed argument in favor of a variable fuel tax.

27. The author of Passage 1 would probably say that the tax credit proposed in Passage 2
    a. is as good as the proposal in Passage 1.
    b. does not address the issue of maintaining a price structure that supports future profits.
    c. should be offered to the consumer, instead.
    d. would be too expensive.
    e. would encourage consumers to burn more gasoline.

28. The main purpose of the third paragraph of Passage 2 is to
    a. argue against a potential alternative strategy.
    b. give a short history of free-market capitalism.
    c. distinguish low prices from price manipulation.
    d. show how the government can encourage innovation.
    e. point out errors made in the past.

29. Which of the following techniques is used by the authors of both passages?
   a. Citing well-known authorities in support of their proposals.
   b. Describing a problem and then describing a possible solution and how it would work.
   c. Attacking people who disagree with their proposals.
   d. Wrapping their proposal in patriotic arguments.
   e. Belittling the ability of government to deal with economic problems.

30. The main purpose of the last paragraph of Passage 1 is to
   a. show that the variable excise tax is the only way to foster renewable fuel development.
   b. show that truck drivers would not suffer under the variable tax proposal.
   c. offer one solution to the problem of uncertain profits slowing development of alternative fuels.
   d. establish a price of $3 a gallon for gasoline.
   e. argue that only government can encourage development of renewable energy sources.

31. The main purpose of the last paragraph of Passage 2 is to
   a. explain what a tax credit is.
   b. offer a solution to the problem of slow development of alternative energy source.
   c. argue in favor of electric vehicles.
   d. give consumers a choice of taxes to pay.
   e. summarize the arguments made in the preceding paragraphs of the passage.

32. Which best characterizes the overall relationship between the two passages?
   a. Both argue for similar approaches to encourage renewable energy development.
   b. Passage 2 rejects the proposal made in Passage 1.
   c. Passage 1 rejects the proposal made in Passage 2.
   d. The proposal made in Passage 1 includes the one made in Passage 2.
   e. The proposal made in Passage 2 includes the one made in Passage 1

Questions 33 – 40 are based on the following passage:

The first photographs were based on the work of the German chemist Johann Heinrich Schulze who, in 1727, discovered that silver nitrate darkened upon exposure to light. The first "photograms" were images made by exposing silver nitrate on paper or metal surfaces. During the nineteenth century, a number of researchers worked to combine this effect with various lenses in order to capture and reproduce images from different sources. The first process for making commercial images was ultimately announced in 1839 by Louis Jacques Mandé Daguerre, a French painter whose name became attached to the product, the daguerreotype.

The daguerreotype quickly became popular in Victorian England, where it was used, principally, for portraits. Today, as photography moves beyond the chemical capture of images onto paper and into the digital era, other applications abound: landscapes, interiors, sports and journalism, to name but a few. And yet, the portrait remains one of the major applications for the technology.

In portraiture, as in other types of photography, the nature and characteristics of light are of the utmost importance. To the photographer, light is a living thing, dynamic and animated. But, whereas in sports or journalism, for example, the photographer must make do with the light conditions he finds when it is time to shoot, light can usually be controlled for a portrait shot. And, good lighting can make all the difference in the world in a portrait, conveying mood, revealing detail, establishing the photographer's style, even making a "mistake" seem like a bit of panache. Understanding light is the creative equivalent of a get-out-of-jail-free card. So much so that the professional portrait photographer expends a great deal of time and money on lights and equipment that will put him in charge.

The various lighted areas of a photograph are described as highlights, mid-tones, and shadows. *Specular* highlights are the brightest spots: direct reflections from the studio lights or strobes. In a portrait they are typically seen in the eyes or on the tip of the nose. From these bright portions, diffused highlights spread gradually into the mid-tones. At the other side of the mid-tonal range, there will be transition areas where the available light fades gradually into the dark shadows. If these transitions are abrupt, narrow areas, the lighting is said to be hard light. Hard light can give a stark effect to portraits and might be used for a craggy-faced coal miner, for example, or for black-and-white shots. Broader transitions produce soft lighting, and lead to a gentler mood. This type of lighting is more suitable for a wedding portrait, for example.

A wide variety of devices are available for producing and modifying the light in a photographic studio. Studio lighting has the advantage of being reproducible, so the skilled photographer can get the same results every time. Modern lighting usually consists of flash units, also called strobes, rather than the hot, power-hungry floodlights that used to be the norm. While this equipment can be elaborate and expensive, it doesn't have to be. A poor carpenter blames his tools, but with practice, one can get great results from a simple setup comprised of two or three lights. Studio lighting setups vary with the preferences of the photographer, but they all have a number of elements in common.

The main light that shines on the subject is called the key light. The camera exposure is determined by the amount of light the key throws upon the subject. The key is usually positioned off to one side of the camera, and will throw shadows across the face from the subject's nose and eyebrows. One or more fill lights may be used to lighten these shadowed areas and reduce image harshness. Fill lights are adjusted to throw half as much light, or less, onto the subject compared to the key. A kicker may be positioned to illuminate the back of the model, creating a halo effect and making the subject stand out from the background. Finally, there may be background lights to illuminate the background directly.

Studio photographers often use modifiers of one type or another to diffuse and soften the light emanating from these sources. Modifiers make the light source effectively larger, reducing shadows and broadening transition areas. The best-known light modifier is the photographer's white umbrella, which can be used to reflect light from the source onto the model, but many other types of modifiers exist. The simplest is a large piece of white cardboard, called a fill card. As with lights, the choice of modifiers is a matter of individual preference, and every studio photographer has his favorite combinations of lights and modifiers for achieving different effects.

Although the basic principles remain the same, the practice of photography has come a long way since the days of the daguerreotype.

33. The main purpose of this passage is
   a. give a history of photography
   b. to show that different photographers have different styles
   c. to compare portraiture with other forms of photography
   d. to contrast modern photography with the daguerreotype
   e. to give an overview of photographic portrait lighting

34. The main purpose of the first three paragraphs (Lines 1-26) is to
   a. explain how daguerreotypes were made
   b. describe the different kinds of photography
   c. provide context for the discussion of portrait lighting
   d. contrast chemical and digital photography
   e. show why sports photography may not have good lighting

35. The word "photogram" is between quotation marks because
   a. it is something that Johann Heinrich Schulze said.
   b. it is a coined term not in common use today.
   c. it is a German word.
   d. the author wants to place emphasis upon it.
   e. it was a way of sending messages with silver nitrate at that time.

36. The phrase "light is a living thing" is an example of
   a. a metaphor.
   b. a simile.
   c. an exaggeration.
   d. an anthropomorphism.
   e. poetic license.

37. The word "mistake" is between quotation marks because
    a. it is something that someone said.
    b. it is a slang expression.
    c. it describes something that may not really be an error.
    d. all photographers make mistakes sometimes.
    e. the author doesn't want to offend anyone.

38. The phrase "Understanding light is the creative equivalent of a get-out-of-jail-free card" is an example of
    a. a metaphor.
    b. a simile.
    c. an attribution.
    d. poetic license.
    e. hybrid vigor.

39. The main purpose of paragraph 4 is to
    a. show the relationship between lighting and mood.
    b. explain the difference between hard and soft light.
    c. tell the reader what kind of lighting to use for a wedding portrait.
    d. define a number of terms used to describe lighting features on photographs.
    e. tell the reader where specular highlights are found.

40. The word "specular" is in italics because
    a. it is a term that is being defined in the sentence.
    b. it is a foreign word.
    c. it is misspelled.
    d. it is a slang expression.
    e. it is a double-entendre.

Physics

1. Which of the following is a vector quantity?
   a. Distance
   b. Speed
   c. Velocity
   d. Time

2. A perfectly circular track has a circumference of 400 meters. A runner goes around the track in 100 seconds instead of her usual time of 80 seconds because a leg cramp causes her to stop running for 20 seconds. What is her average speed?
   a. 0 m/s
   b. 5 m/s
   c. 4 m/s
   d. 20 m/s

3. A space station is revolving in a circular orbit around Earth. Consider the following three statements:
   I. The center of mass of the space station is necessarily located at its geometric center.
   II. The center of mass is moving at a constant velocity.
   III. The center of mass of the space station is moving at a constant speed.
   Which of the following statements is true?
   a. I is true.
   b. II is true.
   c. III is true.
   d. I, II, and III are not true.

4. A box with a weight of 10 newtons is resting on a table. Which statement is true?
   a. The force of the table on the box is the reaction to the weight of the box.
   b. The force of the box on the table is the reaction to the weight of the box.
   c. A 10 newton force on Earth is the reaction force.
   d. There is no reaction force because the system is in equilibrium.

5. Bobsled tracks are flat when they are going straight, but when there is a turn, the track is angled (banked) to create a centripetal force. Assuming no friction, the banking angle is θ, the radius of curvature is r, and the maximum speed the bobsled can have without moving off the track is v. If the radius of curvature is doubled and the banking angle remains the same, which of the following statements is true?
   a. The maximum speed is $2v$.
   b. The maximum speed is $4v$.
   c. The maximum speed is $1.4v$.
   d. The maximum speed depends on the banking angle.

6. The diagram below shows a force F pulling a box up a ramp against the force of friction and the force of gravity. Which of the following diagrams correctly includes vectors representing the normal force, the force of gravity and the force of friction?

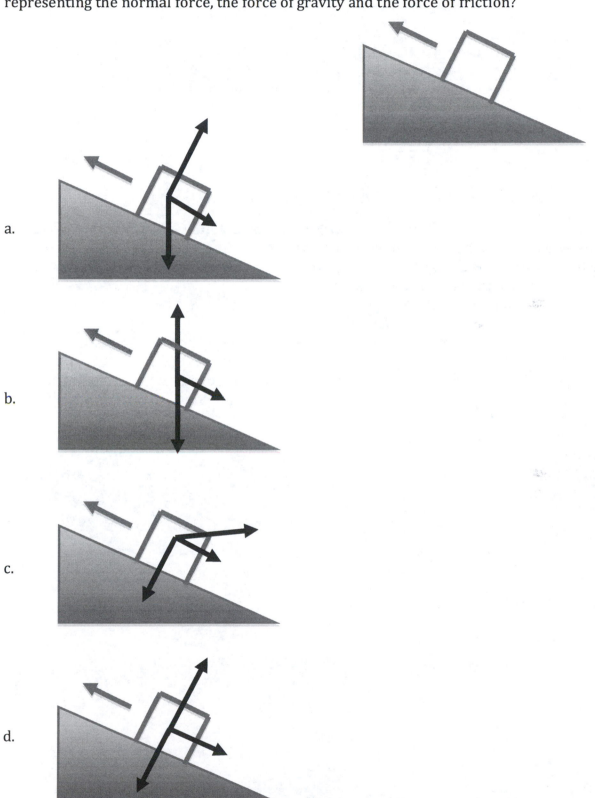

a.

b.

c.

d.

7. A force of 25.0 N pulls three blocks connected by a string on a frictionless surface. What is the tension in the rope between the 4.0-kg block and the 2.0-kg block?

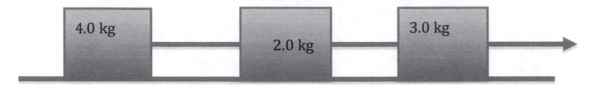

a. 0 N
b. 11.1 N
c. 16.7 N
d. 25 N

8. Suppose a moving railroad car collides with an identical stationary car and the two cars latch together. Ignoring friction, and assuming no deformation on impact, which of the following statements is true?
   a. The speed of the first car decreases by half.
   b. The collision is elastic.
   c. The speed of the first car is doubled.
   d. There is no determining the final speed because the collision was inelastic.

9. A teacher pulls a box across the floor at a uniform speed. He pulls it with a spring scale showing that the force of kinetic friction is 2 newtons. How much total work is done in moving the box 5 meters?
   a. 0 joules
   b. 0.4 joules
   c. 10 joules
   d. 20 joules

10. An athlete's foot is in contact with a kicked football for 100 milliseconds and exerts a force on the football over a distance of 20 centimeters. The force starts at 0 N and increases linearly to 2000 N for 50 milliseconds through a distance of 10 centimeters and then decreases linearly for 50 milliseconds through a distance of 10 centimeters. What is the average power of the athlete's foot while it is in contact with the ball?

    a. 2 kilowatts
    b. 4 kilowatts
    c. 2000 kilowatts
    d. 4000 kilowatts

11. Conservative forces are forces that do not lose energy to processes like friction and radiation and where the total mechanical energy is conserved. Which statement best explains why the work done by a conservative force on an object does not depend on the path the object takes?
    a. This is the definition of a conservative force.
    b. The work done by the force of friction on an object depends on the distance the object moves.
    c. Work can be positive, negative, or zero.
    d. If a force is conservative, any component of the force is equal to the change in a potential energy divided by the change in position.

12. A 100-kg bungee jumper jumps off a bridge, attached to a 20 meter bungee cord. After bouncing around for a minute he finally comes to rest. The stretched cord is now 25 meters long. What is the spring constant of the bungee cord?
    a. 20 newtons per meter
    b. 39 newtons per meter
    c. 49 newtons per meter
    d. 196 newtons per meter

13. A RADAR gun sends out a pulsed beam of microwave radiation to measure the speed of cars using the Doppler effect. The pulsed beam bounces off the moving car and returns to the RADAR gun. For a car that's moving away from the RADAR detector, which of the following statements about the pulsed beam are true?
I. It returns with a longer wavelength.
II. It returns with a shorter wavelength.
III. It returns with a higher frequency.
    a.   I only.
    b.   II only.
    c.   I and III.
    d.   II and III.

14. In resonance, small vibrations can produce a larger standing wave that becomes stronger than the original vibrations, assuming the vibrations are at the right frequency to generate resonance. If a pendulum is vibrated at a resonance frequency, what would you expect to happen?
    a.   The period of the pendulum will increase.
    b.   The time between swings will decrease.
    c.   The pendulum will swing higher.
    d.   The length of the pendulum will decrease.

15. In musical instruments with two open ends, the first harmonic fits one-half wave inside the tube. The second harmonic fits 1 full wave in the tube. The third harmonic fits 1.5 full waves in the tube. Etc. An organ pipe, open at both ends, has a length of 1.2 meters. What is the frequency of the third harmonic? The speed of sound is 340 meters per second.
    a.   142 Hz
    b.   284 Hz
    c.   425 Hz
    d.   568 Hz

16. A submarine sits underwater at a constant depth of 50 meters. Which of the following is true about the submarine's buoyant force?
    a.   It is 0 N.
    b.   It is greater than 0 N but less than the submarine's weight
    c.   It is equal to the submarine's weight
    d.   It is greater than the submarine's weight

17. Suppose you have a pipe of length L and radius r, and a liquid with viscosity η. You also have a sensor to detect the liquid's flow rate, which measures the volume of liquid passing through the pipe per second. If you want to increase the flow rate of the pipe, what changes to L, r and η should you make? Assume that the pressure differential remains constant.
    a.   Increase L, increase r, and decreases η
    b.   Decrease L, increase r, and decreases η
    c.   Decrease L, increase r, and increase η
    d.   Increase L, decrease r, and decreases η

18. A cube of aluminum is placed at the bottom of a deep ocean where the pressure is over 20 atmospheres. What happens to the density of the cube?
   a. It remains the same.
   b. It decreases slightly.
   c. It increases slightly.
   d. It becomes zero.

19. A cube of a substance is 5 centimeters on each side. It is placed in a pressure chamber where the pressure on each surface is $3.0 \times 10^7 \, N/m^2$, causing the density of the cube increases by 0.01 %. Which of the following theories is used to describe this?
   a. Young's Modulus
   b. Shear Modulus
   c. Elastic modulus
   d. Bulk Modulus

20. Which of the following statements about a solid metal sphere with a net charge is true?
   a. If the charge is positive it will be distributed uniformly throughout the sphere.
   b. The charge will be distributed uniformly at the surface of the sphere.
   c. The charge will leave the sphere.
   d. The electric field will be tangent to the surface of the sphere.

21. When is the potential of a point charge with respect to a dipole equal to 0 volts per coulomb?
   a. At the midpoint between the positive and negative charge.
   b. At an infinite distance from the dipole.
   c. At the negative charge.
   d. At the positive charge.

22. An electron is moving in a straight line. Another particle is moving in a straight line parallel to the path of the electron but in the opposite direction. Initially the electron and particle are far apart, but get closer together. When the two particles are in the vicinity of one another, they experience an attractive magnetic force. Which of the following is a correct inference from this fact?
   a. The particle has a north pole and a south pole.
   b. The particle is positively charged.
   c. The particle is negatively charged.
   d. The particle has either a north pole or a south pole.

23. Electromagnetic radiation — also known as light — consists of perpendicularly oscillating electric and magnetic fields. Which of the following statements about electromagnetic radiation is untrue?
   a. The energy of the radiation is determined by the frequency and Plank's constant.
   b. The "color" of light is determined by its wavelength.
   c. Electromagnetic radiation sometimes obeys wave theory.
   d. Electromagnetic radiation sometimes obeys particle theory.

24. Current in an electrical circuit is normally measured in amperes. Which of the following does not represent an alternative way of expressing units of current?
   a. coulombs per second
   b. volts per ohm
   c. electrons per second
   d. Watt-volts.

25. What is the total resistance between points X and Y in the circuit diagram below?

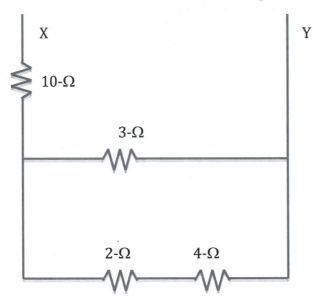

   a. $0\,\Omega$
   b. $12\,\Omega$
   c. $19\,\Omega$
   d. $16\,\Omega$

26. Which is the correct formula for the energy stored in a fully-charged capacitor with capacitance C when its attached to a battery of voltage V?
   a. C/V
   b. ½CV²
   c. CV
   d. 0 volt

27. A 6.0-megaohm resistor is connected in series with a 5.0-microfarad capacitor and fully charged with a 3-volt battery. The battery is disconnected and the capacitor is connected directly to the resistor. How long will it take for the capacitor to fully discharge?
   a. Infinite time
   b. 30 seconds
   c. 0.0333 second
   d. 90 seconds

28. Two beams of light with the same phase and wavelength travel different paths and arrive at the same point. If maximum constructive interference occurs at this point, which of the following statements is true?
   a. The two beams arrive 180° out of phase.
   b. The two beans arrive 90° out of phase.
   c. The lengths of the paths differ by an odd-number of half wavelengths.
   d. The lengths of the paths differ by an integral number of wavelengths.

29. Which of the following statements explains what causes a rainbow?
   a. The components of sunlight strike water droplets at different angles.
   b. Water molecules produce an emission spectrum when sunlight strikes them.
   c. The speed of light in water depends on its wavelength.
   d. There is total internal reflection for certain wavelengths of sunlight.

30. An object is 20 cm in front of a thin convex lens with a focal point of 10 centimeters. Where is the image located?
   a. 10 cm in front of the lens.
   b. 20 cm in front of the lens.
   c. 10 cm behind the lens.
   d. 20 cm behind the lens.

31. Which type of aberration does not occur with concave spherical mirrors?
   a. Astigmatism
   b. Chromatic aberration
   c. Spherical aberration
   d. Distortion

32. Ultrasound imaging, which is used for various medical procedures, including imaging pregnant women, is based on which of the following principles.
   a. Doppler effect.
   b. Echolocation
   c. Infrasonic.
   d. Resonance.

33. What does it mean when someone says that electric charge is conserved?
   a. Like charges repel, and unlike charges attract.
   b. The net charge of an isolated system remains constant.
   c. Charges come from electrons and protons.
   d. Charge can never be created or destroyed.

34. Which of the following is true of an electric dipole?
   a. They don't exist in nature.
   b. The charges are equal in magnitude and both are negative.
   c. The charges have opposite signs and can be unequal in magnitude.
   d. The charges are equal in magnitude and have opposite signs.

35. Which law says the number of electric field lines passing through an imaginary surface is proportional to the net charge inside the surface?
    a. Coulomb's law
    b. Gauss's law
    c. Faraday's law of induction
    d. Biot-Savart law

36. Which of the following is true about a diffraction grating?
    a. The more slits per inch, the greater the amount of destructive interference.
    b. Blue light diffracts more than red light in a diffraction grating.
    c. A diffraction grating produces maxima and minima only for monochromatic light.
    d. Light passing through a diffraction grating produces a bulls-eye pattern.

37. Specular reflection might come occur on a surface like a mirror, while diffuse reflection might occur on a wooden tabletop. Which of the following statements best describes the difference between specular and diffuse reflection?
    a. For diffuse reflection, the angle of incidence is equal to the angle of reflection.
    b. For diffuse reflection, surface irregularities are large compared to the wavelength of visible light.
    c. One hundred percent of the light is reflected for specular reflection.
    d. The conservation of momentum is followed in specular reflection.

38. Two rays parallel to the optical axis of a concave mirror are incident upon the mirror. Where do the two rays intersect?
    a. At a point behind the mirror.
    b. At infinity.
    c. At the center of curvature.
    d. At the focal point.

39. How is light created in the core of the sun?
    a. convection
    b. fission reactions
    c. fusion reactions
    d. chemical reactions

40. A school nurse measures the height of every boy in a school with 1000 pupils and determines that the average height is 1.64 meters with a standard deviation of 0.05 meter. Which of the following statements is true?
    a. Sixty-eight percent of the students have heights between 1.59 meters and 1.69 meters.
    b. There are as many students with heights above 1.64 meters as below 1.64 meters.
    c. More students are 1.64 meters tall than any other height.
    d. None of these statements may be made conclusively.

Quantitative Reasoning

1. If Sara can read 15 pages in 10 minutes, how long will it take her to read 45 pages?
   a. 20 minutes
   b. 30 minutes
   c. 40 minutes
   d. 50 minutes

2. Restaurant customers tip their server only 8 percent for poor service. If their tip was $3.70, how much was their bill?
   a. $40.15
   b. $44.60
   c. $46.25
   d. $50.45

3. If Leonard bought 2 packs of batteries for x amount of dollars, how many packs of batteries could he purchase for $5.00 at the same rate?
   a. 10x
   b. 2/x
   c. 2x
   d. 10/x

4. Choose the algebraic expression that best represents the following situation: Jeral's test score (J) was 5 points higher than half of Kara's test score (K).
   a. J = ½K + 5
   b. J = 2K – 5
   c. K = (J – ½) – 5
   d. K = ½J – 5

5. Enrique weighs 5 pounds more than twice Brendan's weight. If their total weight is 225 pounds, how much does Enrique weigh?
   a. 125 pounds
   b. 152 pounds
   c. 115 pounds
   d. 165 pounds

6. What does (4x – y) + (-10 + y) equal if x = 3 and y = 4?
   a. 2
   b. -2
   c. 22
   d. 14

7. A pasta salad was chilled in the refrigerator at 35° F overnight for 9 hours. The temperature of the pasta dish dropped from 86° F to 38° F. What was the average rate of cooling per hour?
   a. 4.8°/hr
   b. 5.3°/hr
   c. 5.15°/hr
   d. 0.532°/hr

8. Loral received all her grades for the semester (in parentheses) along with the weight for each grade, shown below. What is her final grade?

   <u>Weight</u>

       45% = 3 tests (80%, 75%, 92%)
       25% = final (88%)
     15% = paper (91%)
       15% = 2 oral quizzes each worth 25 points (22, 19)

   a. 88
   b. 86
   c. 79
   d. 85

9. The following items were purchased at the grocery store. What was the average price paid for the items?

Item	Cost	Quantity
Milk	$3.50/carton	2
Banana	$0.30 each	5
Can of soup	$1.25/can	3
Carrots	$0.45/stick	6

   a. $0.34
   b. $0.55
   c. $0.93
   d. $1.38

10. What does 68% equal?
   a. .0068
   b. .68
   c. 6.8
   d. 6800

11. Multiply 2 1/7 x 3 2/3.
   a. 4/7
   b. 1 32/45
   c. 7 6/7
   d. 1 1/3

12. Find $(27 \div 9)$ x $(\sqrt{25}$ x 2$)$.
   a. 90
   b. 12
   c. 45
   d. 30

13. What is the missing number in the sequence: 4, 6, 10, 18, ___, 66.
   a. 22
   b. 34
   c. 45
   d. 54

14. Which of the following is an improper fraction?
   a. 2/3
   b. 1 3/5
   c. 5/2
   d. 2.50

15. Convert 250 centimeters to kilometers.
   a. 0.0025 km
   b. 0.025 km
   c. 0.250 km
   d. 2.50 km

16. Rick renovated his home. He made his bedroom 40% larger (length and width) than its original size. If the original dimensions were 144 inches by 168 inches, how big is his room now if measured in feet?
   a. 12 ft x 14 ft
   b. 16.8 ft x 19.6 ft
   c. 4.8 ft x 5.6 ft
   d. 201.6 ft x 235.2 ft

17. What is $(x^2)^3 \cdot (y^2)^5 \cdot (y^4)^3$?
   a. x^6y^{22}
   b. x^6y^{120}
   c. x^5y^{14}
   d. x^6y^{-2}

18. Simplify the following fraction: $[(x^2)^5 y^6 z^2] / [x^4 (y^3)^4 z^2]$.
   a. $x^{40} y^{72} z^4$
   b. $x^6 y^{-6}$
   c. $x^3 y^{-1}$
   d. $x^{14} y^{18} z^4$

19. There are 64 fluid ounces in a ½ gallon. If Nora fills a tank that holds 8 ¾ gallons, how many ounces will she use?
   a. 560 ounces
   b. 1,024 ounces
   c. 1,088 ounces
   d. 1,120 ounces

20. Shaylee goes shopping for two types of fruit: mangoes that cost $2.00 each and coconuts that cost $4.00 each. If she buys 10 pieces of fruit and spends $30.00, how many pieces of each type of fruit did she buy?
   a. 4 mangoes and 6 coconuts
   b. 5 mangoes and 5 coconuts
   c. 6 mangoes and 4 coconuts
   d. 7 mangoes and 3 coconuts

21. Which of the following values is *not* equal to 12(45 – 8)?
   a. 540 – 96
   b. 12 x 45 – 12 x 8
   c. (-8 + 45) 12
   d. 45 (12 – 8)

22. Which of the following fractions is equal to 4/5?
   a. 8/15
   b. 16/25
   c. 12/15
   d. 28/40

23. A house is 25 feet tall and a ladder is set up 35 feet away from the side of the house. Approximately how long is the ladder from the ground to the roof of the house?
   a. 43 ft
   b. 25 ft
   c. 50 ft
   d. 62 ft

24. Derek received 6 job offers from the 15 interviews he did last month. Which ratio best describes the relationship between the number of jobs he was not offered and the number of jobs for which he interviewed?
    a. 6/15
    b. 15/6
    c. 3/5
    d. 2/3

Use the following table to answer questions 25 – 27.

Mrs. McConnell's Classroom	
Eye Color	**Number of Students**
Brown	14
Blue	9
Hazel	5
Green	2

25. What percentage of students in Mrs. McConnell's classroom has either hazel eyes or green eyes?
    a. 23%
    b. 30%
    c. 47%
    d. 77%

26. How many more students have either brown or blue eyes than students who have hazel or green eyes?
    a. 23
    b. 7
    c. 16
    d. 14

27. What is the ratio of students with brown eyes to students with green eyes?
    a. 1:2
    b. 3:1
    c. 1:5
    d. 7:1

28. What is 4 2/9 ÷ 2 2/3?
    a. 11 7/27
    b. 1 7/12
    c. 1 1/12
    d. 2 5/12

29. On a map, the space of ½ of an inch represents 15 miles. If two cities are 4 3/5 inches apart on the map, what is the actual distance between the two cities?
   a. 138 miles
   b. 39 miles
   c. 23 miles
   d. 125 miles

30. If Louis travels on his bike at an average rate of 20 mph, how long will it take him to travel 240 miles?
   a. 48 hours
   b. 12 hours
   c. 20 hours
   d. 8 hours

31. Maria paid $28.00 for a jacket that was discounted by 30%. What was the original price of the jacket?
   a. $36.00
   b. $47.60
   c. $40.00
   d. $42.50

32. A soda company is testing a new sized can to put on the market. The new can is 6 inches in diameter and 12 inches in height. What is the volume of the can in cubic inches?
   a. 339
   b. 113
   c. 432
   d. 226

33. What is the product of 41.20 and 10.5?
   a. 43.260
   b. 4.326
   c. 43,260
   d. 432.60

34. A garden has a perimeter of 600 yards. If the length of the garden is 250 yards, what is the garden's width?
   a. 25
   b. 50
   c. 175
   d. 350

35. Which of the following values is greatest?
    a. -4 minus 10
    b. -25 – (-30)
    c. 4(-20)
    d. -2(-10)

36. A farmer set up a rain gauge in his field and recorded the following daily precipitation amounts over the course of a week: 0.45 inches, 0.0 inches, 0.75 inches, 1.20 inches, 1.1 inches, 0.2 inches, and 0.0 inches. What was the average precipitation over that week?
    a. 0.74 in
    b. 1.05 in
    c. 0.53 in
    d. 3.70 in

37. 25% of what number is 80?
    a. 200
    b. 320
    c. 160
    d. 135

38. Tony has the following number of T-shirts in his closet:
    White - 5
    Black - 2
    Blue - 1
    Yellow - 3
If Tony's electricity goes out, how many T-shirts would he have to pull out of his closet to make sure he has a yellow T-shirt?
    a. 4
    b. 8
    c. 9
    d. 11

39. While at the airport, Adrienne shops for perfume because the product is duty-free, meaning there is no sales tax. If she makes a purchase of $55.00 and the sales tax in that city is 7%, how much money has she saved?
    a. $3.85
    b. $0.38
    c. $7.85
    d. $4.65

40. Enrique is a full-time employee who earns $12.00 per hour. If he works overtime, he receives time-and-a-half (where each hour worked over 40 hours is compensated at 1.5 times the regular rate). If Enrique works 45 hours, how much money will he earn?
   a. $540
   b. $570
   c. $510
   d. $600

Answers and Explanations

Natural Science

Biology

1. B: Glycogen is a polysaccharide, a molecule composed of many bonded glucose molecules. Glucose is a carbohydrate, and all carbohydrates are composed of only carbon, oxygen, and hydrogen. Most other metabolic compounds contain other atoms, particularly nitrogen, phosphorous, and sulfur.

2. E: Endocytosis is a process by which cells absorb larger molecules or even tiny organisms, such as bacteria, than would be able to pass through the plasma membrane. Endocytic vesicles containing molecules from the extracellular environment often undergo further processing once they enter the cell.

3. A: Because the energy of the products is less than the energy of the substrate, the reaction releases energy and is an exergonic reaction.

4. B: The diploid chromosome number for humans is 46. After DNA duplication but before the first cell division of meiosis, there are 92 chromosomes (46 pairs). After meiosis I is completed, the chromosome number is halved and equals 46. Each daughter cell is haploid, but the chromosomes are still paired (sister chromatids). During meiosis II, the two sister chromatids of each chromosome separate, resulting in 23 haploid chromosomes per germ cell.

5. C: Genes code for proteins, and genes are discrete lengths of DNA on chromosomes. An allele is a variant of a gene (different DNA sequence.. In diploid organisms, there may be two versions of each gene.

6. C: Angiosperms produce flowers, with ovules inside of ovaries. The ovaries become a fruit, with seeds inside. Gymnosperms have naked seeds that are produced in cones or cone like structures.

7. C: Alternation of generations means the alternation between the diploid and haploid phases in plants.

8. C: Plants exchange gases with the environment through pores in their leaves called stomata. Animals exchange gases with the environment in many different ways: small animals like flatworms exchange gases through their skin; insects use tracheae; and many species use lungs.

9. B: Platelets are cell fragments that are involved in blood clotting. Platelets are the site for the blood coagulation cascade. Its final steps are the formation of fibrinogen which, when cleaved, forms fibrin, the "skeleton" of the blood clot.

10. A: HCG is secreted by the trophoblast, part of the early embryo, following implantation in the uterus. GnRH (gonadotropin-releasing hormone. is secreted by the hypothalamus, while LH (luteinizing hormone. and FSH (follicle-stimulating hormone. are secreted by the pituitary gland. GnRH stimulates the production of LH and FSH. LH stimulates ovulation and the production of estrogen and progesterone by the ovary in females, and testosterone production in males. FSH stimulates maturation of the ovarian follicle and estrogen production in females and sperm production in males.

11. B: The gastrula is the first three-layered stage of the embryo, containing ectoderm, mesoderm, and endoderm

12. B: Carbon is released in the form of CO_2 through respiration, burning, and decomposition.

13. A: Pioneer species colonize vacant habitats, and the first such species in a habitat demonstrate primary succession. Succession on rock or lava often begins with lichens. Lichens need very little organic material and can erode rock into soil to provide a growth substrate for other organisms.

14. B: Character displacement means that, although similar, species in the same habitat have evolved characteristics that reduce competition between them. It occurs as a result of resource partitioning.

15. B: Adaptive radiation is the evolution of several species from a single ancestor. It occurs when a species colonizes a new area and members diverge geographically as they adapt to somewhat different conditions.

16. A: The first living organisms probably had not yet evolved the ability to synthesize their own organic molecules for food. They were probably heterotrophs that consumed nutrition from the "organic soup."

17. A: Proteins have a greater diversity of functions than any other biological molecules. It is nucleic acids that encode genetic information: proteins merely carry out the instructions encoded in genes.

18. B: The active site of an enzyme is a uniquely shaped three-dimensional space that is the site of biochemical reactions. Substrates fit within the active site in such a configuration that the enzyme and substrate can bind together. This union is called the enzyme-substrate complex. This pairing is very short lived because as soon as the chemical reaction that the enzyme catalyzes takes place, the enzyme and product dissociate.

19. C: In competitive inhibition, the competitor binds to the same active site as the substrate, preventing the substrate from binding. In feedback inhibition, an end product acts as an inhibitor: the question does not tell you that this has occurred. An allosteric

enzyme has two binding sites, one for substrate (the active site) and one for effector (the allosteric site), and an allosteric inhibitor binds to the latter, not the former.

20. B: The three-dimensional structure of an enzyme is critical for its ability to bind substrates and catalyze reactions effectively. The three-dimensional structure is held in place by hydrogen bonds between amino acids, and these hydrogen bonds are easily disrupted, denaturing the protein (enzyme), by changes in temperature and pH.

21. A: During chemosmosis, energy from light is used to extract electrons from water and pump protons across the thylakoid membrane, creating a creating a proton gradient that powers the generation of ATP and NADPH. Once these molecules are created, they power the processes described in alternatives B-E.

22. E: Short-day plants flower when day length is decreasing or night length is increasing. When plants are exposed to light during the night period, it resets their circadian-rhythm clocks and interferes with their calculation of night length.

23. A: The mouth produces salivary amylase, the enzyme that begins the breakdown of starch into maltose.

24. E: Muscle contraction (shivering) creates heat, so this would not be an effective way of maintaining body temperature in a hot environment.

25. D: A locus is defined as the location of a gene on a chromosome. Alleles of a gene are different forms of the same gene, and they have the same locus. Some alleles may be recessive and some may be dominant.

26. C: If two different traits are always inherited together, they do not segregate in meiosis and are linked.

27. C: A K-selected species has a population size that is constantly at or near carrying capacity. Its members produce few offspring, and the offspring are large and require extensive parental care until they mature.

28. E: Pollution affects the health of ecosystems and can limit population growth, but as it is a byproduct of human activity, it is not dependent on the density of the population.

29. B: Random mating would lead to an equilibrium of allele frequencies, while nonrandom mating (for example, inbreeding or sexual selection) would cause changes in allele frequencies.

30. E: Adaptive radiation is the evolution of several species from a single ancestor. It occurs when a species colonizes a new area and diverges as its members specialize for a particular set of conditions.

31. B: The endosymbiont theory, that early prokaryotes invaded other cells and took up residence there, is based on structure and function of current organelles. The fossil record does not provide direct evidence of this because early microscopic organisms would be unlikely candidates for fossilization.

32. D: DNA is composed of nucleotides joined together in long chains. Nucleotides are composed of a pentose sugar, a phosphate group, and a nitrogenous base. The bases form the "rungs" of the ladder at the core of the DNA helix and the pentose-phosphates are on its outside, or backbone.

33. D: DNA polymerase does not match base pairs with 100% fidelity. Some level of mismatching is present for all DNA polymerases, and this is a source of mutation in nature. Cells have mechanisms of correcting base pair mismatches, but they do not fix all of them.

34. C: The *lac* operon controls transcription of the gene that allows bacteria to metabolize lactose. It codes for both structural and regulatory proteins and includes promoter and operator sequences.

35. C: Plasmids are small circular pieces of DNA found in bacteria that are widely used in recombinant DNA technology. They are cut with restriction enzymes and DNA of interest is ligated to them. They can then easily be used to transform bacteria.

36. B: Although DNA and RNA have the same basic structure, there are some important chemical differences between them. DNA uses deoxyribose as its sugar, while RNA uses ribose. In RNA, the base uracil replaces thymine. RNA can base-pair with itself to form a double stranded molecule; however, it generally is single-stranded.

37. A: If implantation occurs, the embryo secretes HCG. This stimulates the corpus luteum to produce estrogen and progesterone to maintain the pregnancy.

38. E: The head contains a haploid nucleus with 23 chromosomes. The head also contains the acrosome, a lysosome containing enzymes that are used to penetrate the egg.

39. C: If non-disjunction occurs late in embryonic development, only some of the individual's cells will have extra or missing chromosomes, resulting in mosaicism.

40. B: The mother can only be *ii* and the father must be heterozygous because the son is type O.

General Chemistry

1. A: The kinetic energy of the gas molecules is directly proportional to the temperature. If the temperature decreases, so does the molecular motion. A decrease in temperature will

not necessarily mean a gas condenses to a liquid. Neither the mass nor the density is impacted, as no material was added or removed, and the volume remained the same.

2. C: Graham's law of diffusion allows one to calculate the relative diffusion rate between two different gases based on their masses.

3. A: Since there are 7 moles of neon out of a total of 14 moles of gas in the cylinder, the partial pressure of neon will always be 50% of the total pressure, regardless of the temperature.

4. C: The most electronegative atoms are found near the top right of the periodic table. Fluorine has a high electronegativity, while Francium, located at the bottom left on the table, has a low electrongativity.

5. A: Heat is absorbed by the solid during melting, therefore ΔH is positive. Going from a solid to a liquid greatly increases the freedom of the particles, therefore increasing the entropy, so ΔS is also positive.

6. B: Density is determined by dividing the mass of the solution by its volume. The mass is 200 g, and the total volume is 0.2 L, or 200 mL. So 200 g/200 mL = 1 g/mL.

7. D: Acidity increases as we travel down the periodic table with regard to the halogens. Even though fluorine is the most electronegative element and would be expected to stabilize a negative charge well, it is such a small atom that it is poorly able to stabilize the negative charge and therefore will have a stronger bond to the hydrogen. As the atoms get larger, moving from fluorine to iodine, the ability to stabilize a negative charge becomes greater and the bond with the hydrogen is weaker. A stronger bond with the between the halogen and the hydrogen will result in less acidity, since fewer hydrogen ions will be produced.

8. C: Since there are three moles of NH_4^+ per mole of salt and 1 mole of PO_4^{3-} per mole of salt, the total ionic concentrations must be 2.7 M of NH_4^+, and 0.9 M of PO_4^{3-}.

9. D: During osmosis, solvent flows from the lowest to the highest concentration of solute, in this case B to A. The membrane is semi-permeable and only allows the solvent to move, not the solute.

10. D: Using the decay formula, C-14 remaining = C-14 initial$(0.5)^{t/t \, half\text{-}life}$. So, 1 mg $(0.5)^{20000/5730}$ = 0.09 mg. This problem is best solved using the decay formula since 20,000 years is 3.5 half lives. If a student is careful in their reasoning, this problem can be solved without the decay formula. After 3 half-lives, there would be 0.125 mg remaining. If allowed to decay for 4 half-lives, 0.0625 mg would remain. Since only half of this half-life were allowed to elapse, only half of the material would decay, which would be 0.03 mg. Subtracting this amount from 0.125 mg, the amount remaining after 3 half-lives, gives 0.09 mg, which is the amount of material remaining after 3.5 half-lives.

11. C: The mass number is the number of protons and the number of neutrons added together. The number of protons is also known as the atomic number and can be found on the periodic table. Therefore, the number of neutrons is the mass number (238) less the number of protons, in this case, 92, so we have 146 neutrons. The number of electrons always equals the number of protons in a neutral atom, so C is the correct answer.

12. D: Each oxygen has a charge of -2 for a total negative charge of -8. Potassium (K) only exists in compounds as +1. Therefore for the molecule to have a neutral charge, the Mn must be in a +7 oxidation state.

13. B: The nitrogen is missing its lone pair of electrons, and should have two dots above it. A correct Lewis structure shows how the atoms are connected to each other as well as all of the valence electrons in the compound. Each bond represents two electrons.

14. C: Three oxygen are equal to a total charge of -6. Therefore, the two iron atoms must equal that with a positive charge, or +6. So each iron atom must be +3, and the compound is iron (III) oxide.

15. C: 100 g of HBr equals 1.23 moles, and 100 g of Mg equals 4.11 moles. From the coefficients of the balanced equation, the ratio of HBr to Mg is 2:1. This means that to react 1.23 moles of HBr, 2.46 moles of Mg would be required. Since 4.11 moles of Mg are present, Mg is in excess.

16. D: For a general reaction, $a\,A + b\,B \rightarrow c\,C + d\,D$, the equilibrium equation would take the form:

$$K_{eq} = \frac{[C]^c [D]^d}{[A]^a [B]^b}$$

where a, b, c and d are the coefficients from the balanced chemical reaction. Pure liquids and solids are excluded from the equation. Since all reactants and products in the problem are gaseous, the equilibrium equation for the reaction would be:

$$K_{eq} = \frac{[CCl_4][HCl]^4}{[CH_4][Cl_2]^4}$$

17. A: First, one must understand that pK_a is the acidity dissociation number. The larger the number, the less acidic. Acetic acid is a carboxylic acid. When H^+ is given off, a negative charge results on the O. Because there is a second equivalent oxygen bonded to the same carbon, this negative charge can be shared between both oxygen atoms. This is known as resonance stabilization and this conjugate base will be more stable and more of the acid molecules will remain dissociated resulting in higher acidity. For ethanol, when the O-H bond breaks, the negative charge resides completely on the O. It cannot be stabilized by other atoms and therefore reforms the methanol rapidly. This results in very low acidity, since very few protons will be released.

18. C: There are 0.05 mol of sulfuric acid being added, but a total of 0.10 mol of H^+ since sulfuric acid is diprotic (H_2SO_4). This is being added to 0.1 mol of NaOH. The moles of acid and base exactly cancel each other out; therefore the pH of the resulting aqueous solution will be near 7.

19. D: In I, dissolving a solid into a liquid breaks up the organized solid matrix, therefore increasing disorder. III converts single particles into two particles, and in IV, solid ice sublimes into a gas. Both of these processes also increase disorder and thus, entropy. II is a decrease in entropy, since 7 molecules, with 3 being gaseous, are reacted to form 2 solid molecules.

20. A: B is 1-butanol, since its longest chain of carbons is 4, not 3. C is 3-pentanone, since there are 5 carbons in the chain and it is a ketone, rather than a carboxylic acid. D is 1-butene, not 3-butene. The name should be assigned by giving the double bond the lowest number.

21. A: NMR, or nuclear magnetic resonance, allows one to determine the connectivity of atoms in an organic molecule, by "reading" the resonance signals from the attached hydrogen atoms. IR, or infrared spectroscopy, can help to identify the functional groups that are present, but does not give much information about its position in the molecule. Mass spectrometry breaks apart a large molecule and analyzes the masses of the fragments. It can be useful in analyzing protein structure. HPLC, or high performance liquid chromatography, is a method used to separate a mixture into its components.

22. D: The fact that ΔG for the reaction is negative indicates the reaction is spontaneous. This does not mean the reaction will be faster or slow. Diamonds as we all know do not rapidly convert to graphite, and in fact do so only very slowly, over millions of years, thank goodness.

23. B: The carbon of a carboxylic acid has three bonds to oxygen atoms and one to a carbon atom. The carbon bonded to the carboxylic carbon will have an oxidation state of zero. Each oxygen atom will have an oxidation number of -2. However, one oxygen is bonded to a hydrogen, which will have an oxidation number of +1. This results in a total oxidation state of -3 for both oxygens bonded to the carbon. Therefore, since the carbon must balance the oxidation states of the oxygens (-3) and the carbon (0), the oxidation state of the carbon must be +3. The three bonds to oxygen give a +3, and the bond to carbon is 0.

24. D: Mendeleev was able to connect the trends of the different elements behaviors and develop a table that showed the periodicity of the elements and their relationship to each other.

25. D: Different molecules must have the same chemical formula to be isomers. They differ only in which atoms are bound to which. Having the same molecular weight does not necessarily mean two molecules have the same formula.

26. C: Proteins are large polypeptides, comprised of many amino acids linked together by an amide bond. DNA and RNA are made up of nucleic acids. Carbohydrates are long chains of sugars. Triglycerides are fats and are composed of a glycerol molecule and three fatty acids.

27. C: Normality refers to the concentration of acid equivalents (H^+ ions), not the concentration of the solute. 100 g of phosphoric acid has a MW of 98 g/mol. So, 100g/98 g/mol = 1.02 moles of phosphoric acid are in solution. The total volume of the solution is 0.4 L, so the molarity of the solution is 1.02 mol/0.4 L = 2.55 M. Since there are three acid equivalents for every mole of phosphoric acid, the normality is 3 x 2.55 = 7.65 N.

28. A: Communities around the world who drink fluoridated water have shown dramatic decreases in the number of dental cavities formed per citizen versus those communities that do not drink fluoridated water.

29. A: Density is mass per volume, typically expressed in units such as g/cm^3, or kg/m^3.

30. B: Acids and bases will react violently if accidentally mixed, as will reducing and oxidizing agents.   Both reactions can be highly exothermic and uncontrollable.

Organic Chemistry

1. A: The number of carbon and hydrogen atoms corresponds to the general formula for alkanes, C_nH_{2n+2}. This indicates that the compound is saturated and there are no double bonds to any carbon atoms. There can therefore only be single bonds involving the C and O atoms, which is satisfied only if the compound is an alcohol (one of thirteen possible isomers) or an ether (thirteen other possible isomers). Aldehydes and ketones have a double bond between a carbon atom and an oxygen atom and therefore cannot have a formula that agrees with the formula $C_6H_{14}O$.

2. D: The formula contains six carbon atoms and six hydrogen atoms. Structure a) corresponds to the formula C_6H_{12}. Structures b) and c) correspond to C_6H_8. Only structure d) of these possibilities corresponds to the formula C_6H_6.

3. B: In this reaction, the electron-rich C=C bond of 1-methylcyclohexene accepts a proton from the strong acid solution forming a C-H bond between one of the C=C carbon atoms and the H^+ ion. This results in the formation of a 2° carbonium ion at C2 if the C-H bond forms on C1 or a 3° carbonium ion at C1 if the C-H bond forms on C2. The process is a reversible equilibrium, and since a 3° carbonium ion is more stable than a 2° carbonium ion, any 2° ions formed would rearrange to the 3° ion structure. Addition of H_2O to the 3° carbonium ion, followed by loss of H^+, produces the product 1-methylcyclohexanol.

4. A: This is the definition of the carbonyl functional group. The term "carbonyl" refers specifically to the C=O group. The other three each contain a carbonyl group, but are not of themselves a carbonyl group. The carbonate group is the CO_3^{2-} ion, and the term

"carbonate" is used to refer to salts and esters of the corresponding carbonic acid. The carboxylic function is the –COOH group. The acyl group is the carboxylic function without the -OH and can be represented by RCO. It is a carbonyl bonded to a carbon group (R). Ketones, aldehydes, esters and amides all contain acyl groups.

5. A: Optical isomers are properly termed enantiomers; molecules whose structures are exact mirror images of each other but that cannot be superimposed on each other. Such molecules have no planes or axes of symmetry, and are therefore asymmetric. An optically active compound may have only one isomer or it may have many. The number of possible isomers depends on the number of asymmetric carbon atoms in the molecule.

6. C: Enantiomeric isomers, or enantiomers, are molecules that are identical in every respect but are non-superimposable mirror images of each other according to the orientation of substituents about a central atom.
Geometric isomers are compounds that differ in their geometric structure only, for example, *cis-* and *trans-*2-butene.
Conformational isomers are the different shapes that can be adopted by a molecule, for example, the *chair*, *twist* and *boat* conformations of the cyclohexane molecule.
Structural isomers are compounds with the same molecular formula but different molecular structures, for example, C_2H_6O, which represents either ethanol, CH_3CH_2OH, or dimethyl ether, CH_3OCH_3.

7. A: Multiple bonds between two atoms bind the two together more tightly, bringing them closer together physically. Thus, they have shorter bond lengths. The total bond energy of a multiple bond is at minimum the sum of the energies of the individual bonds that make up the multiple bond. Therefore, they have higher bond energies according to their multiplicity. For example, the bond lengths and energies of bonds between carbon atoms follow the order:
C-C < C=C < C≡C
longest   shortest
Multiple bonds are sites of increased reactivity in molecules, especially as they are the defining feature of many different functional groups.
Bond lengths and energies are not relevant to molecular weights.

8. C: Chromatography of a tangible quantity of some mixture of compounds is used to separate those compounds from each other so that they can be collected in pure form. Small-scale chromatography is often used in laboratory procedures to monitor the progress of a reaction, usually through the disappearance of a compound as the reaction or other process progresses over time.

9. A: Caffeine is an alkaloid compound and therefore contains nitrogen. The –ine ending of the name indicates the presence of a nitrogen atom in the compound. The molecular structure shown contains no nitrogen and therefore cannot possibly be that of caffeine. The IUPAC name of the compound is 2-cyclohexyl-5-methylhept-4-en-3-one. It is, however, a

conjugated enone, because the C=C bond and the C=O bond are separated from each other by a single C-C bond.

10. A: The C=O bond stretching absorption appears in IR spectra in the range of 1760 – 1670 cm^{-1}.
The CN bond absorption of nitriles appears in the range 2260 – 2220 cm^{-1}
The C-O-C bond absorption of ethers appears in the range 1260 – 1000 cm^{-1}.
The C=C bond absorption of alkenes appears in the range 1680 – 1640 cm^{-1}.

11. B: The mechanism of a reaction in which a nucleophile displaces another from an sp^3 carbon atom with inversion of the stereochemistry of the other three substituents is called a bimolecular nucleophilic substitution reaction. The mechanism is indicated by the S_N2 tag.
An S_N1 reaction proceeds by loss of a nucleophile from a molecule, forming a carbonium ion intermediate.
The E1 and E2 reactions are elimination reactions and not substitution reactions.

12. C: In all forms of chromatography, the separation of components in a mixture is achieved by the differential rates at which the compounds adsorb and desorb from the surfaces of the stationary phase particles. The more times this can happen as the mixture progresses down the column, the better the separation of the components.
Solubility plays a role in chromatography but does not solely determine the separation of the components.
Similarly, polarity plays a role in chromatography but does not solely determine the separation of components.
Absorption is a different process than adsorption and is not involved in chromatography.

13. A: Sugar molecules are polyhydroxy aldehydes and ketones in their linear forms. They can form a cyclic structure by an intramolecular reaction that produces a cyclic hemiacetal or hemiketal structure. These cyclic structures are either five- or six-membered oxygen-heterocyclic rings. They are not bicyclic.
Sugar molecules can bond together very easily and are often found naturally in that form, like sucrose, starches and celluloses. Simple sugars that are naturally crystalline are easily recrystallized. Others tend to be thick, syrupy liquids rather than crystalline solids.

14. B: Grignard reagents are formed by the reaction of alkyl and aryl halides with magnesium metal in an anhydrous oxygenated solvent such as diethyl ether or tetrahydrofuran. A radical mechanism splits the carbon-halogen bond in such a way that the alkyl or aryl radical and the halogen radicals coordinate to a magnesium atom to form alkyl (or aryl) magnesium halide.
A Grignard reaction occurs when an appropriate Grignard reagent is reacted with a substrate molecule, such as a carbonyl compound. Grignard reactions are used to add structures to other molecules.
Magnesium bromide ($MgBr_2$) is one of the disposable by-products of Grignard reactions.

15. A:

Et₂O

Br + Mg ──→ MgBr

1 – (2-methylpropyl)

Cyclohexyl 2-methylpropyl ether

1 – Bromocyclohexanol

Cyclohexyl 2-methylpropanoate

16. D: All three are different names for the same compound produced by this reaction.

17. A: The lone pair electrons on the N atom of an amide are stabilized by delocalization into the carbonyl group π system. The orbital hybridization of the N atom is thus stabilized as $sp^2 + p$, which has trigonal planar geometry. Rotation about the amide C-N bond is restricted by the p orbital overlap.

18. B: Phosphines do not add to imines and phosphine oxides do not add to the carbonyl group.
The Wittig reaction involves the attack of the carbonyl group of a ketone or aldehyde by a phosphinium ylide, which results in the production of an alkene and a phosphine oxide byproduct. Typically, a triphenyl phosphinium ylide is used as a Wittig reagent. The carbon group of the Wittig reagent forms the double bond of the alkene in the same location as the carbonyl of the reactant ketone or aldehyde.

19. B: The Williamson synthesis produces ethers by the reaction of sodium alkoxides and alkyl halides. The reaction proceeds via an S_N2 mechanism. The alkoxide is produced by treatment of an alcohol with a very strong base such as sodium hydride to extract the –OH proton. An alkyl halide is then added to the solution, and the alkoxide ion nucleophile displaces the halide to form the ether product.

20. A: All steroids have the 6-6-6-5 ring structure in answer a). The other three structures are not steroidal, although they do have some similarities.

21. B: An annulation reaction forms a ring structure in a molecule. This may be a new ring on an existing ring. A bicycloannulation reaction forms two ring structures in a molecule,

by joining one part of the molecule to two other parts of the same molecule in the same step. The reaction can be used to form complete three-dimensional tricyclic structures.

A "double addition" reaction occurs when two addition reactions are involved in a single reaction during a synthesis.

A "coordination reaction" occurs when an organometallic coordination compound or complex is formed.

22. D: All of these compounds possess a nitrogen-containing ring in their structures, so all are nitrogen heterocycles.

23. A: Amine oxides are very polar and have a bare oxygen atom bonded to the amine N atom. They are often used as surfactants. Oximes are imines in which the imine N atom has an –OH group bonded to it.

Imines and epoxides do not have bonds between N and O. Imines have a C=N double bond, and epoxides have a three-membered oxygen-heterocyclic ring structure.

Pyrans and furans are six- and five-membered oxygen heterocyclic rings and do not contain N atoms in their structures.

Cyanates are the functional group written as $-OC\equiv N$, with a terminal N atom, and isocyanates are written as $-N=C=O$, with a terminal O atom. Although both contain N and O, neither have a nitrogen-oxygen bond.

24. D: Nitriles are characterized by the presence of a carbon-nitrogen triple bond. Addition of H_2O to this bond produces a hydroxyimine, or oxime, analogous to an enol, which then rearranges to form an amide.

25. B: Polymers in their solid state fracture conchoidally like glass. As they are heated and become more plastic, they attain a state in which they lose the ability to fracture like glass. The temperature range in which this physical property transition takes place is known as the "glass transition temperature", T_g. At temperatures below T_g, fracturing is observed, and at temperatures above T_g it is not observed.

26. D: Trimyristin and tristearin are "triesters" of glycerol, myristic acid and stearic acid. Base-catalyzed hydrolysis, or saponification, must return all three of these materials.

27. A: Diols and dicarboxylic acids undergo condensation reactions to produce linear polyesters. Glycerol has three –OH groups rather than two, and can therefore form ester links to more than one diacid molecule. This results in the formation of cross-linked polyesters.

Diglycerides and triglycerides are the diesters and triesters formed by reaction of diols and triols with monocarboxylic acids.

Saccharides are carbohydrate "sugar" molecules.

Polyethers do not contain an ester linkage.

28. D: Plasticizers are incorporated into the physical structure of a polymer and act to keep the polymer molecules separated. This provides flexibility or "plasticity" to the polymer.

Stabilizers are compounds added to prevent destructive reactions such as oxidation from occurring.

Adjuvants are typically unreactive materials added to a polymer in order to impart certain properties such as color.

Block copolymers are polymers that are composed of a long section, or "block", of one type of monomer and then joined to another block composed of a different type of monomer.

29. C: Glucose molecules are formed by photosynthesis and used in the formation of starch and cellulose biopolymers.

Fructose is a simple sugar found in fruits and vegetables.

Galactose and galactulose are epimeric forms of glucose.

30. C: "Plastic" means that the shape of the material can be changed by pressure alone.

"Thermoplastic" means that a polymeric material becomes plastic when heated.

"Thermosetting" means that the material becomes solid when heated, as the heating process promotes the formation of cross-linking bonds.

"Thermonuclear" refers to the energetic activation of reactions between atomic nuclei through extreme heating.

"Neoplastic" is a term used to describe a cancer growth.

Reading Comprehension

1. A
2. D
3. B
4. C
5. B
6. B
7. D
8. D
9. A
10. C
11. A
12. A
13. B
14. C
15. B
16. C
17. A
18. B
19. D
20. D
21. A
22. C

23. D
24. B
25. E
26. C
27. B
28. A
29. B
30. C
31. B
32. B
33. E
34. C
35. B
36. A
37. C
38. A
39. D
40. A

Physics

1. C: Vectors have a magnitude (e.g., 5 meters/second) and direction (e.g., towards north). Of the choices listed, only velocity has a direction. (35 m/s north, for example). Speed, distance and time are all quantities that have a size but not a direction. That's why, for example, a car's speedometer reads 35 miles/hour, but does not indicate your direction of travel.

2. C: The average speed is the total distance (400 m) divided by the total time spent travelling (100 s). Answer A would be correct if the question asked for the instantaneous velocity while the runner was stopped. Ans. B is the runner's average speed when running at her usual time, finishing the race in 80 seconds. Answer D is the average speed if the runner had completed the race in 20 seconds, not 100.

3. C: In a uniform gravitational field, such as occurs near Earth's surface, an object will move like a point mass located at the center of mass. However, this does not necessarily mean that the geometrical center of an object is the same as its center of mass, depending on its shape, design and mass distribution. The center of mass of a sphere or cube is at its geometric center because you can imagine the sphere as consisting of a large number of point masses located at certain points in space. Multiplying the point masses by their location and dividing by the total mass gives the center of mass. I is not true because the space station may not be completely symmetrical. III is true because the space station is undergoing uniform circular motion around Earth. If the orbit had been elliptical, this would not be true because the speed would have changed depending on the station's position. However, even though the speed is constant in a circular orbit, the velocity is not.

Since velocity has a direction associated with it, and the space station is moving in a circular path, its velocity is constantly changing.

4. A: Newton's third law is that if object A exerts a force on object B, then object B exerts and equal and opposite force on object A. This means for every action (force) there is a reaction (force in opposite direction). The box is in equilibrium because the force of the table on the box is equal and opposite to the force of gravity (weight) of the box pushing against the table. Since the force of the box against the table is an action force (caused by gravity), the reaction force would be the table pushing back against the box.

5. C: Centripetal force can be expressed as $F = m(v^2/r)\cos\theta$. Increasing the radius effectively decreases the force unless you also increase the velocity. By assuming that the maximum centripetal force remains constant, you can increase the maximum speed v by as much as $\sqrt{2}$. Any higher and the v^2 term will be too high for the new radius.

6. A: The force of gravity points straight down. The normal force is perpendicular to the surface of the block. The force of friction points down the slope. The only one of these diagrams with all three vectors pointing in those directions is Answer A.

7. B: Using Newton's second law $F = ma$, the acceleration of all three blocks, which have a combined mass of 9 kg, is $a = 25$ N $/ 9$ kg $= 2.78$ m/s^2. The force pulling the rear block is $F = ma = 4$ kg x 2.78 m/s$^2 = 11.1$ N. Another way of thinking of this is the tension represents 4/9 of the total force, since the total mass is 9 kg and the rear block has a mass of 4 kg. This must equal the tension on the rope pulling on that block. Answer C is the tension of the string connecting the 3 kg and 2 kg masses. Answer D is the tension on the rope pulling all 3 masses.

8. A: A collision is considered elastic when neither object loses any kinetic energy. Since the cars latch together, this can't be the case. You could easily prove this by calculating the cars' $KE = \frac{1}{2}mv^2$. If the railroad cars had bumpers instead of couplers, the moving car would stop and transfer all its momentum and kinetic energy to the stationary car, causing an elastic collision. In a closed system like this one, however, the conservation of momentum is an absolute law, where an objects' momentum is its mass times its velocity. There are no external forces acting on the two cars. The only forces are between the two cars themselves. The momentum before the collision is the same as the momentum after the collision: $mv_{initial} + m(0$ m/s$) = mv_{final,} + mv_{final}$. So $mv_{initial} = 2mv_{final}$, and $v_{initial} = 2v_{final}$. Thus the final velocity is half the initial velocity.

9. A: Since the box is moving at a uniform speed, the net force on the box is 0 newtons. Thus the work $(W = Fd)$ is also 0 joules. Answer C incorrectly assumes that 2 newtons of force are used to move the box 5 meters, and while it's true that the teacher is pulling with 2 newtons, the frictional force counteracts this. Answer D incorrectly assumes the work performed by the teacher and the work due to friction add together for a net work of 20 newtons. Answer B incorrectly uses $W = F/d$. The vertical forces acting on the box—gravity and the normal force—also have a net force of 0 newtons and work of 0 joules.

10. A: In addition to understanding power, this problem requires you to understand unit conversions. The power P is the work divided by the time, and the work here is the average force times distance. Since the force increases evenly from 0 to 2000N and decreases at the same rate, the average force is 1000N. Keeping in mind that 20 cm = 0.2 m and 100 milliseconds = 0.1 seconds, this means P = 1000N x 0.2 m / 0.1 s = 2000 watts or 2 kilowatts.

11. D: Answers A, B, and C all shed light on what conservative forces are but do not answer the question of why the work on an object doesn't depend on its path. Friction is a force that causes kinetic energy to be lost and where the amount of loss depends on the path taken. Work can be expressed in multiple ways, including as the sum of potentials, and all that matters is the beginning and ending position. Think of this in terms of gravity, gravitational potential energy, and the work done by gravity. In this case, $W = \Delta PE = mg\Delta h$, where h is an objects height. Dividing work by the change in position shows $mg = \Delta PE / \Delta h$. Since mg is a force, you can say $F = \Delta PE / \Delta h$, or the force equals the work/change in potential energy divided by its change in position.

12. D: The jumper's weight is 9.8 m/s² x 100 kg= 980 Newtons. Insert the weight—a force—into the equation F = kx, where k is the spring constant and x is the displacement from rest of the spring. The displacement here is 5 meters. 20 meters is unnecessary information, and just a measure of how long the spring is, not how far it was displaced. k = F/x = 980 N / 5 meters = 196 N/m.

13. A: The Doppler effect shows that light/radiation from a object moving away has a longer wavelength. A car moving towards the RADAR gun would have a shorter wavelength. Since c = vf (where c = speed of light, v = wavelength and f = frequency), increasing the wavelength would cause the frequency to become smaller.

14. C: As the amplitude of the pendulum increases due to resonance, it will swing higher. However, the period of a pendulum is not connected to how high it swings. Only the length of the pendulum affects its period. Obviously, the length of a pendulum will not be affected by how high it's swinging or whether it's in resonance.

15. C: Three full waves fit into the pipe, according to the question description. The wavelength of the third harmonic in this pipe organ is 1.2m/1.5 waves = 0.8 m. Using the wave equation ($v = \lambda f$), f = 340 m/s / 0.8 m = 425 Hz.

16. C: If the sub stays at a constant depth, its buoyant force must be equal to its weight. If the buoyant force was larger, it would rise. If lower, it would sink. All objects underwater experience a buoyant force, so it cannot be zero.

17. B: To increase the flow rate, you'd want to: (1) reduce the length L of the pipe, (2) make the pipe wider, and (3) have a fluid with low viscosity (just think of how much slower a viscous fluid like molasses runs as compared to water). Answer B is the only answer that describes all of these changes.

18. C: In a vacuum the only forces acting on the molecules of aluminum are other aluminum molecules. Inside a fluid, the molecules of the fluid collide with the sides of cube and exert a force on the surface causing the cube to shrink in size slightly. Also, the temperature of water deep in the ocean is very low. This causes the vibratory motion of the aluminum molecules to decrease, which decreases the dimensions of the cube.

19. D: The bulk modulus describes a substance's reaction to being squeezed and its change in volume, which directly affects its density. The elastic modulus is the ratio of stress to strain for an object. Young's modulus deals with the elasticity and length of an object. The shear modulus deals with the elasticity of a shape and the stress that's applied perpendicular to its surfaces.

20. B: Concerning answer A, if an object has a positive charge, it is because electrons were removed. In the case of a conductor, the electrons will migrate away from the surface, leaving a positive charge on the surface. The electric field of a negative point charge points towards the charge. The electric field of a sheet of charges will be perpendicular to the sheet.

21. B: The electric potential, which comes from the electrostatic potential energy, is the potential of a charged particle in an electrical field. The stronger the field or the higher the charge, the higher the potential. So putting a point charge near a dipole will create a potential, depending on how strong the dipole's field is. For a potential of 0, you would need to be far from the dipole, so its electric field strength was effectively 0. At an infinite distance from a dipole, the distance between the charges is approximately 0 meters, so the net charge is 0 coulombs.

22. B: A moving electron produces a circular magnetic field that is perpendicular to the velocity of the particle. Since the magnetic field produced by the electron exerts a magnetic force towards the electron, the charge on the particle is positive. This conclusion requires the correct application of the right-hand rule for the creation of a magnetic field by a current (thumb in the direction of the velocity of a positive charge with fingers curling in the direction of the magnetic field) and the right-hand rule for the magnetic force on a moving charge (fingers in the direction of the positively charged particle's velocity, thumb in the direction of the magnetic force, and palm in the direction of the magnetic field). Answer D is wrong because there are no particles with only a north pole or a south pole. There may be a force between the electron and the particle if the particle is a tiny magnet, but the direction of the force would depend on the magnet's orientation, and hence answer A is wrong.

23. B: Although the wavelength of light is related to its color, the frequency really determines light's color. For example, light slows down when it enters water. This doesn't change the frequency or the color of light, but it does change its wavelength. The fact that light sometimes acts like a wave and sometimes acts like particles is called "duality." The

energy of light can be expressed as E = hv, where h is the Plank's constant and v is the frequency.

24. D: Current can be expressed as the flow of charge per time, which Answers A and C both express. Answer B follows from the units in Ohm's law, V = IR. Answer D is the only incorrect way of expressing current, although watts per volts would be an OK way to express amperes, which follows from the Power equation P = IV.

25. B: For resistors in series, the total resistance is the sum of their individual resistances. For resistors in parallel, the total resistance is given by $1/R = 1/R_1 + 1/R_2 + ...$ First, the bottom two resistors have a total resistance of 2 Ω+ 4 Ω= 6 Ω. Then add this in parallel with the 3 Ohm resistor. 1/R = 1/3 + 1/6 = 1/2. So R = 2 Ω for the bottom three elements. To find the total resistance, add this in series to the top resistor, for a total R = 10 Ω + 2Ω = 12Ω.

26. B: Answers A and C are wrong because they doesn't have the units of energy (joules). To make things easier, the correct answer follows the same form as other kinds of energy (KE = ½mv2, a spring's potential energy is ½kx², etc.) The capacitance is defined as Q/V, so the energy is proportional to QV. The potential at a point in space is determined by the concentration of charge at that point, but the potential difference (V = work/charge) is defined in terms of the motion of a small test charge. At the very beginning of the process of charging up a capacitor, the work needed to move a test charge from the positive plate to the negative plate is 0 volts. As the capacitor charges up, more energy is required to move the charge because the charge is repelled by the negative plate. The total energy stored is Q × average voltage. Since the voltage increases linearly, the average voltage is ½ V.

27. A: The current that flows in the resistor connected to the battery without the capacitor is 5×10^{-5} ampere. When the battery is disconnected this is the initial current as the electrons flow from the negative plate through the resistor to the positive plate. As electrons build up on the positive plate, the current decreases. The decrease is exponential, so the capacitor never fully loses its charge. Answer B is the time constant for the RC circuit (resistance × capacitance). After 30 seconds, the current is 37% of its initial value. When the time lapsed is three times RC, the current will be reduced to 95%. Within a short time, the current will be so small it will not be measurable with an ammeter, although it will technically never fully discharge.

28. D: For constructive interference, the waves must arrive having the same phase. Therefore, neither Answers A or B can be correct. Constructive interference occurs when the waveforms add together, producing a maximum that is twice as intense as either of the individual waves. Answer C would cause the waves to be out of phase by 1, 3, 5 or 7 (etc.) half-wavelengths, meaning the waves would be out of phase by a half-wavelength. Only Answer D assures that the two waves arrive in phase.

29. C: A ray of sunlight consists of many different colors of light. The speed of red light in water is slightly larger than the speed of violet light, so the angle of refraction of violet light

is greater than that of red light. This causes the light to separate and creates a spectrum of colors, like in a prism. Raindrops do exhibit total internal reflection for all the wavelengths inside the droplet, although this is not what causes the rainbow. Instead, this causes a second refraction as the sunlight emerges from the water droplet, which can sometimes been seen in nature as a "double rainbow."

30. D: Since the lens is convex, the focal length is positive and the image will appear behind the lens. You can use the lens equation to solve this. $1/f = 1/o + 1/i$, where f is the coal length, i is the image location and o is the object location. Since the object is in front it has a positive sign. $1/10$ cm $= 1/20$ cm $+ 1/i$, so $1/i = 1/20$ and $i = 20$ cm. The positive sign for the image means that it is behind the lens.

31. B: This question is asking about a concave MIRROR, not a lens. Since light does not pass through a mirror—it only reflects off of it—the different colors of light all bend the same amount. If light was passing through a lens, the different colors would bend slightly different amounts, causing chromatic aberration. That's not the case here. Spherical aberration occurs because the focal point of the mirror changes slightly as you move away from the center (optical axis). Astigmatism occurs when incident rays are not parallel to the optical axis. A circular beam, striking a lens or mirror at an angle to the optical axis, will become a parabola. Distortion concerns magnification and occurs in both mirrors and lenses.

32. B: Medical ultrasound machines use echolocation, in which sound waves are bounced off objects and the returning sound waves are used to create an image. This same process is also used by some animals, such as bats and dolphins. The spectrum of sound has three areas: infrasonic, audible, and ultrasonic. Humans can hear sound waves between 20 Hz and 20,000 Hz, so these are the cut-off points. The Doppler effect refers to the changing pitch of sound for objects that are moving towards or away from you.

33. B: Although Answer A is also true, Answer B correctly states the law of conservation of charge. Answer C is only partially true because there are other elementary particles with a charge. Answer D is false because a photon will produce an electron-positron pair. There is also the example of a proton and electron combining to form a neutron.

34. D: Dipoles -- meaning two poles -- are either electric or magnetic, but represent a simple a pair of opposite charges with equal magnitude. Just as a magnet cannot have only one pole, many physicist believe it's impossible to have a mono-pole, which has only one pole. Dipoles are important in chemistry because many molecules, water for example, are polarized. The charges in nonpolar molecules are uniformly distributed throughout the molecule. The oxygen side of a water molecule has a net negative charge and the hydrogen side has a net positive charge because the charges are not uniformly distributed.

35. B: This is Gauss's law, which concerns electric field lines. Electric field lines leave positive charges and enter negative charges. Electric field lines entering a surface are positive and electric field lines leaving a surface are negative. If there is no charge inside

the surface, the sum of the electric field lines is zero. Coulomb's law refers to attractive force between any two charged particles. Faraday's law regards the creation of electric fields from moving magnetic fields. The Biot-Savart law concerns the creation of magnetic fields from moving charges.

36. A: Diffraction gratings produce so much destructive interference that large distances separate the bright lines due to interference. This means diffraction gratings can be used to separate light consisting of different wave lengths. Answer B is wrong because blue light, which has a shorter wavelength than red light, refracts and diffracts less than red light. The greater the wavelength of light, the more it changes direction when it hits an edge.

37. B: Specular reflection occurs with smooth surfaces such as mirrors or a water puddle. All of the light is not necessarily reflected because there can be refraction and absorption. Answer A is wrong because a rough surface consists of many smooth surfaces oriented in different directions, so the light will not necessarily reflect at the same angle as incidence. Note, however, that for each small surface on a rough tabletop, for example, the angle of incidence is equal to the angle of reflection.

38. D: Parallel rays striking a concave mirror intersect at the focal point. If the rays weren't parallel — say they were both coming from an object near the mirror — then they would intersect elsewhere, depending on the focal length and their distance from the mirror. For example, Answer B would be correct if the rays both started at the focal point. For an object between the focal point and the mirror, the virtual image is created by extending the rays geometrically behind the mirror. The center of curvature is at the center of the sphere that defines the spherical mirror and is equal to twice the focal length.

39. C: Sunlight consists of photons and cosmic rays. Sunlight is produces when hydrogen, deuterium, and tritium nuclei combine to form helium. This nuclear reaction is called fusion. Fission occurs when a nucleus disintegrates into two smaller nuclei. In both fission and fusion, energy is released because the binding energy per nucleon increases. This decreases the mass of the nuclei.

40. D: Because you do not know the exact distribution of heights, Answer D is correct. The deviation of a measurement is the difference between the mean (average measurement) and the measurement. The standard deviation is the square root of the mean of the deviations squared. On average, about 68% of a sample will fall within one standard deviation. So if the standard deviation is 0.05 meters, ABOUT 68% of the students will stand between 1.64 +/- 0.05 meters. But this is only true if you have a fairly normal distribution of values. Similarly, this does not mean that half of the students are necessarily taller or shorter than the average. Since it is an average, you could have a class with a 20-foot giant and seven 5-foot-tall students and have an average that is a fairly large 6.857 feet. Answer C refers to the Mode, which looks for the most popular value.

Quantitative Reasoning

1. B: The relationship can be expressed as: $15/10 = 45/x$; $15x = 450$; $x = 30$.

2. C: The total amount of the bill is: $3.70/x = 8/100$; $370 = 8x$; $x = \$46.25$.

3. D: First set the relationship up and solve for the number of packs: $x/2 = 5/\text{packs}$; $x(\text{packs}) = 10$; $\text{packs} = 10/x$.

4. A: The correct expression is: $J = 1/2K + 5$.

5. B: If $E + B = 225$, and $E = 2B + 5$, then $225 - B = 2B + 5$. Solving for B, $3B = 220$ and $B = 73.3$. $225 - 73.3 = 151.7$.

6. A: Plugging in x and y, you get $(4(3) - 4) + (-10 + 4)$, which is $8 + (-6)$, or $8 - 6 = 2$.

7. B: The average rate of cooling is: $(86º - 38º) / 9$ hrs; $48º / 9 = 5.33º$ F per hour.

8. D: Calculate the weighted average of the 3 tests: $(80+75+92) / 3 = 82.3$; Calculate the average of the 2 oral quizzes: $(22/25) \times 100 = 88$ and $(19/25) \times 100 = 76$, so $(88 + 76)/2 = 82$. Multiply each grade by their weight, and then add them all up to determine the final grade: $(82 \times .45) + (88 \times .25) + (91 \times .15) + (82 \times .15) = 85$.

9. C: Calculate the average price as $[(3.5 \times 2) + (0.3 \times 5) + (1.25 \times 3) + (0.45 \times 6)] / (2 + 5 + 3 + 6) = 0.93$.

10. B: $68\% = 68/100$. To express as a fraction, move the decimal two places to the left, $.68$.

11. C: $2\ 1/7 \times 3\ 2/3 = 15/7 \times 11/3 = 165/21 = 7\ 18/21 = 7\ 6/7$.

12. D: Remember the order of operations: $(27 \div 9) = 3$ and $(\sqrt{25} \times 2) = 10$; $3 \times 10 = 30$.

13. B: Double the number that is added to the previous number. So, $4+2=6$, $6+4=10$, $10+8=18$, $18+16=34$, and $34+32=66$.

14. C: An improper fraction is one whose numerator is greater than the denominator.

15. A: 1 kilometer is equal to 100,000 centimeters. $250/10000 = .0025$.

16. B: $144 \times 0.40 = 57.6 + 144 = 201.6$ and $168 \times 0.40 = 67.2 + 168 = 235.2$; then, convert to feet: $201.6/12 = 16.8$ ft and $235.2/12 = 19.6$ ft.

17. A: $(x^2)^3 = x^{(2 \times 3)} = x^6$; $(y^2)^5 = y^{(2 \times 5)} = y^{10}$; $(y^4)^3 = y^{(4 \times 3)} = y^{12}$; $y^{10} \cdot y^{12} = y^{(10+12)} = y^{22}$.

18. B: $(x^2)^5 y^6 z^2 / x^4 (y^3)^4 z^2 = x^{(2 \times 5)} - x^4 = x^{10} - x^4 = x^6$; $y^6 - y^{(3 \times 4)} = y^6 - y^{12} = y^{-6}$; $z^2 - z^2 = z^0$ or 0; so the answer is: $x^6 y^{-6}$.

19. D: 1 gallon = 128 ounces, so 8 x 128 = 1,024 ounces for 8 gallons. ½ = 64 gallons, and ¼ = 32 gallons, so 64 + 32 = 96 ounces to fill the ¾ gallons; the total ounces required is 1,024 + 96 = 1,120 ounces.

20. B: If mangoes are represented by x and coconuts are represented by y, then:
$x + y = 10$, and $2x + 4y = 30$
$2(10-y) + 4y = 30$
$20 - 2y + 4y = 30$
$2y = 10$
$y = 5$ and $x = 5$, or 5 of each type of fruit

21. D: $12(45 - 8) = 540 - 96 = 444$, but $45(12 - 8) = 540 - 360 = 180$.

22. C: The least common multiple of the fraction 12/15 is 3, lending 4/5.

23. A: Using the Pythagorean theorem: $25^2 + 35^2 = c^2$. $625 + 1225 = c^2$. $c = \sqrt{1850} = 43.01$.

24. C: The number of jobs he did not get is 15 – 6 = 9. The ratio is 9:15 or 3:5.

25. A: Total # of students = 14 + 9 + 5 + 2 = 30. 5 + 2 = 7. 7/30 = X/100. 700 = 30X. X = 23.3.

26. C: 14 + 9 = 23 and 5 + 2 = 7. 23 – 7 = 16.

27. D: Brown eyes = 14 and Green eyes = 2. So, the ratio is 14:2 or 7:1.

28. B: 4 2/9 = 38/9 and 2 2/3 = 8/3. 38/9 ÷ 8/3 = 38/9 x 3/8. 114/72 = 57/36 = 19/12 = 1 7/12.

29. A: ½ / 15 = 4 3/5 / X; ½ X = 15 x 23/5. ½ X = 69. X = 69 x 2 = 138.

30. B: 20/1 = 240/X. 20X = 240. X = 240/20 = 12 hours.

31. C: If X represents the original price of the jacket and Y represents the discounted amount, then 0.30X = Y and X – Y = 28; X – 0.30X = 28; 0.70X = 28; X = 28/.70 = 40.

32. A: $V = \pi r^2 h$. V = 3.14 x (3^2) x 12. 3.14 x 9 x 12 = 339.12.

33. D: The decimals are counted as 3 spaces from the right, so 41.20 x 10.5 = 432.600.

34. B: The equation for perimeter (P) = 2L + 2W. So, 600 = 2(250) + 2W. Solve for W: 600 – 500 = 2W. 100 = 2W. W = 50.

35. D: Multiplying a negative number by another negative number yields a positive number, in this case -2 x -10 = +20, which is the largest answer choice.

36. C: (0.45 + 0.0 + 0.75 + 1.20 + 1.1 + 0.2 + 0.0) / 7 = 0.53.

37. B: (0.25)X = 80. X = 80/0.25. X = 320.

38. C: He would have to pull out at least 9 (5 + 2 + 1 + 1) to make sure he has a yellow one.

39. A: 55 x 7/100 = 55 x .07 = 3.85.

40. B: He gets paid $12.00/hr for the first 40 hrs: 12 x 40 = $480. For time-and-a-half: 5 x 1.5 = 7.5. 7.5 x 12 = $90. So, 480 + 90 = $570.